# Criminal Justice

# Recent Scholarship

Edited by
Marilyn McShane and Frank P. Williams III

A Series from LFB Scholarly

# Prisonization
## Individual and Institutional Factors Affecting Inmate Conduct

Wayne Gillespie

LFB Scholarly Publishing LLC
New York 2003

**Library of Congress Cataloging-in-Publication Data**

Gillespie, Wayne.
  Prisonization : individual and institutional factors affecting inmate
conduct / Wayne Gillespie.
     p. cm. -- (Criminal justice)
Includes bibliographical references and index.
  ISBN 1-931202-52-4 (alk. paper)
  1. Prisons--United States--Case studies. 2. Prison
administration--United States--Case studies. 3. Deviant
behavior--Labeling theory--Case studies. I. Title. II. Criminal justice
(LFB Scholarly Publishing LLC)
  HV9471 .G555 2002
  365'.6--dc21
                                    2002010423


ISBN 1-931202-52-4

Printed on acid-free 250-year-life paper.

Manufactured in the United States of America.

# Table of Contents

*v*

# CHAPTER 1

# Contextual Research in Corrections

Prison is a context that exerts its influence upon the social relations of those who enter its domain. Clemmer (1940) was one of the first criminologists to recognize that the prison is a community replete with distinctive norms and folkways. Sykes (1958) proposed that inmates form a society of captives bound together by the extreme deprivations imposed upon them by the dominant sociocultural order. Garabedian (1963) suggested that inmates adopt unique social roles in order to function within the prison counterculture. Prisonization involves the extent to which prisoners adopt norms that are indicative of the inmate subculture, and it is the general social process to which these different researchers were referring. The antecedents of prisonization include both the deprivations that inmates encounter inside prison as well as the individual characteristics and differences imported from the outside (Thomas, 1971). Consequently, inmates may express this prisonized normative orientation through maladaptive behaviors such as self-mutilation, suicide, rebellion, and resistance (Matthews, 1999).

Just as the context of a neighborhood, community, or society shapes the interactions that develop therein, so too does the structure of a prison influence the social processes that occur inside. In particular, the antecedents of prisonization include both the individual traits of inmates and the contextual features of correctional institutions. For instance, inmates may encounter interpersonal problems inside prison that lead to prisonization. However, the structure or administration of a prison may present contextual or situational problems that also contribute to prisonization. Thus, the antecedents of prisonization operate at two levels of analysis: the individual (i.e., the micro-level) and the contextual (i.e., the macro-level).

The goal of the present study is to explore the social processes of institutional life, such as prisonization and general misconduct, from a multilevel perspective. The extent to which both the individual attributes of prisoners and the contextual features of prisons influence social processes on the inside is a key issue. In particular, an integrated theory of prisonization is developed that incorporates individual and contextual effects into one parsimonious design using multilevel data from over 1,000 inmates in 30 prisons across Kentucky, Tennessee, and Ohio. Akers (1997) suggests that parsimony, scope, testability, empirical validity, usefulness, and policy implications are all criteria that must be considered when evaluating theory. Each of these standards is addressed by the present study. The analysis ultimately speaks to the merit of the prisonization hypothesis as a worthwhile orienting schema in the study of institutional life.

## The Traditional Model of Penal Consequentialism

Prisonization is a basic learning theory that involves antisocial or maladaptive changes in normative and behavioral patterns in response to physical or social hardships encountered during incarceration. This logic is consistent with a traditional penal philosophy that emphasizes the prosocial consequences of incarceration (i.e., crime prevention). The traditional model of penal consequentialism was both the primary moral justification and the dominant correctional philosophy during most of the twentieth century (Von Hirsch, 1998; Von Hirsch, 1985). It was especially influential in the 1950s and 1960s when many scientific investigations of prison life were well underway.

Rehabilitation was the main preventive goal of penal consequentialism. Rehabilitation involves resocializing inmates in order to change their motives for offending. As Von Hirsch (1998) has noted "the judge was supposed to fashion the disposition to promote the offender's resocialization" (p. 660). Correctional programs associated with the rehabilitative ideal include, but are not limited to, vocational training, academic instruction, general behavior modification, drug and alcohol treatment, and psychological counseling. The central theme of rehabilitation and its contemporary revisions (i.e., peacemaking) is personal change (Braswell & Gillespie, 1998). Both rehabilitation and prisonization entail resocialization. However, while the rehabilitative ideal emphasizes an offender's ability to change in a prosocial direction, the prisonization hypothesis predicts that offenders are just as likely to change in an antisocial manner, particularly during their imprisonment.

Rehabilitation and prisonization are thus flip sides of the same coin; the logic behind each is based upon a conceptualization of human nature that emphasizes the potential for personal transformation.

Yet, in the mid-1970s, the very logic of traditional penal philosophy was attacked. The rehabilitative ideal withered in light of several critical reviews that questioned the effectiveness of rehabilitation programs (Allen, 1981). After an extensive review of correctional research, Martinson (1974) remarked that "these data, involving over two hundred studies and hundreds of thousands of individuals as they do, are the best available and give us very little reason to hope that we have in fact found a sure way of reducing recidivism through rehabilitation" (p. 49). His analysis provided critics of rehabilitation with prized buzzwords: nothing works.

In spite of the evidence that has mounted against the traditional model in recent years, the tenacity of the rehabilitative ideal persists (Cullen, Skovron, Scott, & Burton, 1990; Gendreau, 1998). For instance, Cullen et al. (1990) examined rehabilitation, punishment, and protection as the three main emphases of the criminal justice system. They gauged public opinion to determine support for rehabilitative programs in prison. Cullen et al. (1990) discovered that the public supported rehabilitation (i.e., 54.7 percent) as the main function of prisons, followed by protection (i.e., 35.3 percent) and punishment (i.e., 5.7 percent). The majority of subjects in Cullen et al.'s sample supported rehabilitative, correctional goals. However, a sizeable portion of their sample also favored protection as a primary function of modern corrections.

Indeed, fear of crime and protection from dangerous criminals are familiar rhetoric in modern politics (Caplow & Simon, 1999; Chernoff, Kelly, & Kroger, 1996). According to Von Hirsch (1998), this law-and-order perspective "manifested in the plethora of drastic penal responses being enacted in the United States (and some other countries) today" (p. 660). From this perspective, imprisonment is justified because it decreases the chances that an offender will recidivate by separating him from the community as long as he remains a risk. In other words, incarceration prevents crime by simply incapacitating motivated offenders.

Caplow and Simon (1999) agree that the main explanation for the dramatic population growth in U.S. prisons during the last two decades involves changes in penal policy. They attribute the causes of recent penal policy changes to a combination of factors. During an era of fractioned politics, crime control policy (i.e., the law-and-order perspective) has broad public appeal. Politicians understand that election often rests on a platform that favors hardline punishments for offenders (Caplow & Simon, 1999; Chernoff, Kelly, & Kroger, 1996). Caplow and Simon (1999) maintain that two changes in American political ideologies contributed to the centrality of crime as a political issue. First, they note that social welfare programs are no longer credible. Caplow and Simon (1999) remark that "the loss of confidence in social welfare programs has removed an important set of responses that politicians (both liberals like Lyndon Johnson and conservatives like Richard Nixon) could one use to confront social problems" (p. 70). In the absence of proactive remedies to modern social problems, today's elected officials endorse reactive solutions (i.e., law-and-order criminal justice policy). The politics of punishment are no longer subordinate to the politics of welfare (Caplow & Simon, 1999).

The contemporary American political scene has changed in other ways as well. Specifically, conflicts over values and identities have replaced traditional materialist concerns in modern politics. Consensus is limited on issues such as abortion, gay and lesbian rights, and religion in schools. Caplow and Simon (1999) note that "politicians seeking to build viable majorities inevitably look to the few issues that can bring people together in the new political landscape" (p. 71). Crime control has proved to be an issue that draws widespread consensus.

For example, during the 1988 United States Presidential race, the Bush campaign focused on the case of Willie Horton. Horton committed a violent crime while on a prison furlough program in Dukakis' home state of Massachusetts. Kappeler, Blumberg, and Potter (1996) suggested the following:

> The ad campaign had a devastating effect on the governor of the state, Michael Dukakis, in his presidential election bid. ... It portrayed a violent crime, a weapon, committed by a stranger, who was sent to prey on society by a soft criminal justice system (p. 33).

These political catalysts, combined with other factors such as the unintended consequences of the War on Drugs and greater reflexivity of the penal system, have resulted in public policies that ultimately are creating tremendous growth in the extent of imprisonment in the United States (Caplow & Simon, 1999).

## The Extent of Imprisonment in the United States

The number of people incarcerated each year in the United States has been steadily increasing since the 1980s. According to Blumstein and Beck (1999), the number of inmates in state and federal prisons increased by as much as 260 percent from 315,974 prisoners in 1980 to 1,138,984 in 1996. The United States Department of Justice reports that the number of inmates in state correctional facilities alone increased from 708,393 in 1990 to 1,231,475 in 1999, indicating a gain of about 74 percent. In particular, 15,317 prisoners were under the jurisdiction of state or federal correctional authorities in Kentucky at the end of 1999. Ohio had 46,842 inmates in state and federal correctional facilities, and Tennessee reported 22,502 incarcerated individuals under state and federal auspices in 1999 (Bureau of Justice Statistics, 2000).

Blumstein and Beck (1999) examined these trends and uncovered the primary contributor to the current population growth in U.S. prisons. They analyzed changes in the following areas: offending rates, arrests per offense, commitments to prison per arrest, and time served in prison. Blumstein and Beck (1999) partitioned the prison population growth among these four stages and examined trends separately for drug and non-drug offenses. Then, they examined both drug and non-drug offenses together.

The main forces affecting the growth in imprisonment for drug offenses differed from the dominant factors influencing increased incarceration for non-drug crimes. Blumstein and Beck (1999) determined that both higher arrest rates and increased commitments per arrest are the dominant forces affecting the growth in incarceration for drug offenses. In contrast, they found that the main factors raising incarceration for non-drug offenses appear to be both longer periods of time-served and increased commitments per arrest. Thus, increases in the overall crime rate cannot account for the growth in incarceration for both non-drug and drug offenses.

However, when both drug and non-drug offenses are examined together, the primary contributor to current growth in the U.S. prison population appears to be longer periods of time served (Blumstein & Beck, 1999). Blumstein and Beck (1999) remark that "the preponderance of the responsibility for prison population growth lies in the sanctioning phase, the conversion of arrests into prisoners and the time they serve in prison" (p. 55). They also maintain that changes in criminal justice policy have contributed to the growth of time served. Ultimately, legislation that calls for hardline sentences (e.g., "three strikes" laws, sentencing enhancements, and mandatory-minimum laws) and protracted durations until parole (e.g., "truth in sentencing" laws) contribute to more time served, which in turn has fueled the current population explosion in American prisons. Along with this increased captive population comes heightened expenses as well.

## The Cost of Imprisonment in the United States

As the U.S. prison population grows, the costs associated with imprisonment increase as well (Hagan & Dinovitzer, 1999). Expenditures for state prisons grew from $6,778,000,000 in 1985 to $22,033,000,000 in 1996, representing an increase of 225 percent (Bureau of Justice Statistics, 1999). However, Maguire and Pastore (1997) estimate that the cost of corrections in the United States today is actually closer to $32 billion than $22 billion. Eckl (1998) notes that from the 1980s to the late 1990s state corrections budgets tripled, and these costs surpassed all other state expenditures to become the fastest growing state spending category. Logic seems to dictate that as more men and women are imprisoned each year, the incarceration costs would increase as a function of the additional space needed to house new inmates.

However, when increased housing and construction costs are compared with prison population growth, there appears to be some disparity. In 1984, it cost taxpayers $16,300 per year on average to house one inmate in a state institution; the figure had increased to $20,100 by 1996. The growth in housing costs represents an increase of about 23 percent. For roughly the same period (i.e., from 1980 to 1996), the U.S. prison population grew by 260 percent. Additionally, the number of beds in state and federal prisons grew only 41 percent in the 1990s (Bureau of Justice Statistics, 1997). Again, for roughly the same time frame (i.e., from 1990 to 1999), the population of incarcerated individuals grew by 74 percent. Thus, increases in housing costs do not seem to correspond to the growth in the U.S. prison population.

Additionally, the dollar amount allotted to construction that might accommodate the population growth in U.S. prisons does not appear to be a substantial part of the overall state fiscal expenditures. For instance, of the total state correctional expenses for 1996, only 808,400 dollars went toward prison construction. That represents only 4 percent of the total state prison expenditures for 1996 (Bureau of Justice Statistics, 1999). In fact, at year end 1999, 22 states indicated operating at 100 percent or more of their highest prison capacity (U.S. Department of Justice, 2000). The lack of funds dedicated to construction and housing most likely exacerbates crowding in state institutions. In sum, although the financial costs of incarceration are extremely high, housing expenditures do not seem to be keeping pace with this trend.

## The Contextual Research Project

### Statement of the Problem

Both the extent and cost of imprisonment in the United States are currently growing at unprecedented rates. In fact, incarceration costs now surpass educational funding in some localities within the U.S. (Ambrosio & Schiraldi, 1997). Hagan and Dinovitzer (1999) note that "several large states now spend as much or more money to incarcerate young adults than to educate their college-age citizens (p. 130). Likewise, Walker, Spohn, and DeLone (1996) determined that more African Americans were under correctional supervision (e.g., jail, prison, probation, and parole) than were enrolled in college in 1992. Yet, while the college experience is markedly different from that of imprisonment, the two do share one similarity. Both involve learning within a particular context.

However, the degree to which imprisonment directly affects individuals is still a matter of considerable debate in correctional research. In particular, psychological studies have not been very successful at uncovering the detrimental effects of imprisonment (Bonta & Gendreau, 1990; Bukstel & Kilmann, 1980; Haney, 1998; Toch, 1984). Bonta and

Gendreau (1990) conducted a meta-analysis of studies that examined the psychological well-being of inmates in response to prison crowding, health risks, long-term incarceration, solitary confinement, short-term detention, and death row. They found only inconclusive evidence as to the detrimental, psychological effects of incarceration. In a review of 90 experimental, psychological studies, Bukstel and Kilmann (1980) concluded that imprisonment was not harmful to all individuals. They noted that some inmates deteriorated in response to confinement, but others did not. Toch (1984) summed up the psychological study of imprisonment when he remarked that "we must freely admit at this point that we do not know how long-term inmates react to prison" (p. 511). Yet, despite their own inconclusive findings, psychologists have suggested important directions for future research in corrections.

Specifically, social scientists now stress the influence of context on inmate behavior (Haney, 1997; Wooldredge, Griffin, & Pratt, 2001). For instance, Toch (1984) insisted that many researchers ignore individual and group differences when studying prison life. Different prison contexts may influence how groups of inmates react and adapt to institutional conditions. Likewise, Bonta and Gendreau (1990) advocate a "situation-by-person" approach to correctional research. In particular, they note that researchers should explore individual adaptations and examine more closely the moderating and contextual antecedents of inmate adjustment. Haney's (1997) comments also seem to favor contextual analyses of prison life:

> Notwithstanding the tendency among researchers to talk about prison as if it were some sort of Weberian ideal type, conditions of confinement can vary dramatically along critical dimensions that render one prison a fundamentally different place in which to live from another. Indeed, the effects of confinement in, say, a relatively well run Canadian prison cannot be generalized to those suffered in a dangerously overcrowded or brutally mismanaged U.S. prison (Haney, 1997, p. 531).

In sum, correctional researchers now recognize the importance of context on behavior and advocate future research that incorporates contextual and individual variables into one explanatory model.

This contextual analysis of prison life is based on the assumption that there is significant homogeneity within groups of prisoners and significant heterogeneity between groups of prisoners. As such, the very mechanism that Toch (1984) accused most researchers of avoiding (i.e., individual and group differences) is exploited in this project. In fact, a relatively new methodological technique is used to examine the social hierarchy of prison life. Hopefully, by accounting for the interdependency of prisoners within correctional institutions, the influence of context on the social processes and relationships inside prison will become clearer. In sum, the individual qualities of prisoners and the contextual features of prisons that influence social processes on the inside are considered integral to understanding prisonization and subsequent misconduct.

## Objectives of the Project

The current project has two main objectives. First, a model of prisonization that integrates components from both the importation and deprivation theories of subcultural formation is specified. Early studies of prisonization were theoretically divided concerning the etiology of inmate subculture (Mattingly, 2001; Thomas, 1971). According to indigenous influence theory (i.e., deprivation), the inmate subculture originates internally; importation theory maintains that this subculture has external origins. Specifically, deprivation theorists argue that the inmate subculture forms within prison in response to, or as a function of, the problems and frustrations that inmates encounter on the inside (see Goffman, 1961; Sykes, 1958). Deprivation studies of prisonization focus on prison-based factors such as the length of time served, the frequency of outside contacts, and the number of friendships formed inside prison (see Atchley & McCabe, 1968; Clemmer, 1940; Thomas, 1971; Wheeler, 1961).

Cultural drift theory (i.e., importation), on the other hand, proposes that the inmate subculture is simply an extension of the criminal, street subculture (Irwin, 1980). Importation studies of prisonization usually examine non-prison determinants such as race, gang involvement, and prior attitudes about the law. However, Thomas (1971) proposed that this dichotomy is most likely false; he suggested integrating both perspectives into one analytical model. As such, both theories of subcultural formation (i.e., importation and deprivation) are combined in the present study. At the inmate level, variables from the deprivation perspective include sentence length, the amount of time served, the number of outside contacts, the number of friendships formed inside prison, deviant prison associates, a scale that measures situational problems encountered inside prison, and an inmate's perception of crowding. Age, race, prior incarcerations, prior violence, and prior gang involvement are all included as importation variables.

The second goal of this project involves a multilevel test of this integrated model of prisonization. To date, only one multilevel study has examined the influence of prison contexts on individual processes and social relationships inside prison (see Wooldredge, Griffin, & Pratt, 2001). Thus, the present study is somewhat exploratory and involves several methodological stages. First, hypotheses testing whether prisonization and general institutional misconduct vary across different prisons are enumerated. It is expected that the effects of different micro social processes (e.g., situational problems, differential associations, gang involvement, etc.) on prisonization will vary across institutions. Moreover, the normative orientation of prisonization should predict general misconduct inside prison. Lastly, macro (i.e., institutional) characteristics are added to the model to account for both the variation of prisonization and misconduct across prisons and the variable effects of micro predictors on these two social processes.

Four general expectations guide this multilevel model of prisonization. First, both prisonization and general misconduct should vary across different prison contexts. Second, the effects of some micro social processes on prisonization and misconduct should also vary across institutions. Third, prisonization should be a significant predictor of general institutional misconduct. Fourth, prison features such as crowding, high security, and gang presence should exacerbate the effects of individual-level social processes on prisonization and misconduct.

Importance of the Project

A contextual analysis of prison life is important for several reasons. First, in a time of dramatic population growth in U.S. prisons, a multilevel model highlights the characteristics of prisons that interact with individual determinants to produce maladaptive normative and behavioral patterns. For example, institutional crowding may heighten the effects of individual problems and frustrations on prisonization and other social processes.

Prisonization has been linked to adjustment problems that occur upon release (Clemmer, 1940; Homant, 1984; Peat & Winfree, 1992). Therefore, it is reasonable to speculate that underfunded, overcrowded conditions may cultivate maladjustment among ex-convicts that ultimately results in higher rates of recidivism and increased rates of incarceration. Such institutional conditions (i.e., crowding, funding, etc.) may merit revision or reform if the interactions between the prison and the inmate are problematic in the extreme.

Second, the results from this study may either challenge or confirm traditional and contemporary justifications for imprisonment. In particular, the concept of prisonization is consistent with a traditional penal philosophy (i.e., re-socialization or rehabilitation) that focuses on personal change and examines the consequences of incarceration. While some research (e.g., see Bonta & Gendreau, 1990; Bukstel & Kilmann, 1980; Martinson, 1974) questions the effects of imprisonment, the current project should illustrate exactly how incarceration affects individuals both in terms of norms and behaviors.

Third, this multilevel approach adds to and refines extant scholarship in corrections and criminal justice. Specifically, the individual determinants of prisonization are usually examined independently of contextual features. Correctional researchers, including psychologists, now recognize the importance of institutional context. The present study includes both individual and contextual variables in a statistically appropriate model.

Limitations of the Project

Several limitations must be acknowledged at the outset of this project. First and foremost, the current study is cross-sectional. Many social phenomena occur over time. That is, processes such as prisonization have a temporal element that is difficult to capture with data collected at a single point in time. Longitudinal data are preferable to cross-sectional information when attempting to measure a temporal process. However, early researchers of prisonization used cross-sectional designs to approximate temporal states (Atchley & McCabe, 1968; Wheeler, 1961). As such, this research is consistent with previous studies of prisonization and institutional processes.

Also, given the fact that the selection of inmates into the study was not completely random, some bias may exist in the sample. In order to establish a stronger intraclass correlation (i.e., a measure of homogeneity within groups and heterogeneity between groups), inmates who had continuously served at least six months at any one of the sampled prisons were given the exclusive opportunity to participate in the study. Thus, subjects had to meet a residency requirement in order to participate; inmates at a very early phase of incarceration were excluded.

Lastly, this project is based on survey methodology. Self-report data may not be extremely accurate for multiple reasons. Often, social desirability affects individual responses. In particular, Thomas (1971) enumerated several unique problems with inmate samples. For instance, inmates may be apprehensive about the possibility that the research members are agents of prison administration or the parole board. Some prisoners may believe that if they provide accurate information, it will hurt their chances of parole. Other inmates have no interest in academic research and do not understand how the survey questions are connected to either their own well-being or prison reform in general. However, as Thomas (1971) noted "once adequate rapport was established [with inmates] the major problem was in getting away from the interview rather than in getting the interview started" (p. 45). Likewise, the quality of prisoner self-reports have been verified by several independent research endeavors (Farrington, 1973; Marquis & Ebener, 1981; Petersilia, 1977; Sobell & Sobell, 1978).

For instance, Marquis and Ebener (1981) surveyed male inmates in three states to determine the strengths and weaknesses of self-report data. They compared self-report accounts of arrests and convictions information from official records. Marquis and Ebener (1981) reached the following three conclusions:

-- On the average, prisoners do not deny arrests and convictions. Amounts reported in the questionnaire are usually equal to or greater than the amounts coded from the records.
-- Response reliability is moderately high for self-reports of convictions, but uncertain for reports of arrests.
-- Discrepancies between survey and record values are not predicted well by ability, memory, and demographic variables, so we did not identify the "kinds" of prisoners prone to lying or to other response errors (p. v).

These results are encouraging, given the sensitive nature of conviction and arrest information (Marquis & Ebener, 1981). It is reasonable to believe that if prisoners did not falsify these events during self-report, then they most likely would not distort information concerning other normative and behavioral patterns.

## Summary of the Project

Given the current law-and-order orientation of criminal justice in the United States, it is likely that imprisonment will remain a popular sentencing disposition. Incapacitation is as important a goal as rehabilitation in contemporary corrections. The U.S. prison population will most likely continue to escalate. Subsequently, the costs of imprisonment will also increase. Yet, the manner in which imprisonment actually affects inmates is unclear (Bonta & Gendreau, 1990; Bukstel & Kilmann, 1980; Martinson, 1974; Toch, 1984). Individual and group differences appear to influence the degree to which imprisonment is detrimental. Correctional researchers now advocate contextual analyses of prison life that examine the effects of institutional conditions on the social processes and relationships that occur on the inside (Haney, 1997; Wooldredge, Griffin, & Pratt, 2001).

The current project incorporates individual and contextual elements into one parsimonious model. Specifically, two social processes that occur inside prison (i.e., prisonization and general misconduct) are examined. The main argument is based on the premise that inmates within the same prison are homogeneous while prisoners from different institutions are heterogeneous. Both the similarities within groups and the differences between groups are the result of exposure to differential prison contexts. If this assumption holds, then prisonization is not a universal response to incarceration in all correctional facilities. Likewise, the antecedents and consequences of prisonization should vary from prison to prison. The context of prison exerts a powerful influence upon the social relations that occur inside the walls.

# CHAPTER 2

# Sociological Foundations for Correctional Research

Public interest in penology and corrections developed long before imprisonment became a subject of sociological inquiry. In fact, the rationale for the first penitentiary (i.e., the Walnut Street jail) in the United States was based on religious doctrine rather than scientific research. Bacon (1985) noted that the Quakers were instrumental in converting the Walnut Street jail into an experimental institution where prisoners could perform penance for their crimes. As part of their contrition, prisoners were separated from each other and confined in solitary cells. The Quakers believed that prisoners could be reformed if they were given the opportunity to meditate about their past sins and resolve to live a better life. This correctional approach became known as the Pennsylvania system. The optimism surrounding the Pennsylvania system persisted for a few decades, but eventually waned in light of continuing failure (Johnson, 1997).

A new penology emerged in the nineteenth century that supposedly was free of the sentimentalism of the prior era (Platt, 1977). The National Prison Congress of 1870 advocated a scientific approach to correctional work. However, nineteenth century penology lacked scientific objectivity. In fact, Platt (1977) has argued that nineteenth century penologists were elitist and classist. They viewed prisoners as evolutionary throwbacks who comprised an anti-social class of individuals (see Giddings, 1895; Lombroso & Ferrero, 1895). Furthermore, Platt (1977) criticized the new scientific penology of the nineteenth century (e.g., Wines' treatise on prisons and child-saving institutions) for lacking innovation and simply blending conventional wisdom, religious dogma, and reformist vigor. Thus, nineteenth century penologists, as well as eighteenth century reformers, perceived imprisonment through very subjective lenses that obstructed any objective, scientific analysis of prison life.

The first truly scientific studies of imprisonment began in the early years of the twentieth century. Haynes (1948) noted that three developments contributed to this scientific approach. First, academics began visiting prisons for the purpose of scientific research rather than for humanitarian reasons. For example, Thomas Osborne volunteered to spend a week in Auburn Prison as an inmate for academic study in 1913 (Haynes, 1948). Osborne's experience was the first of its kind and attracted publicity that brought the prison problem to the attention of this country. The exercise also proved to be an early example of participant observation.

Changes in penal policy after 1918 seemed to be the second catalyst that lead to more scientific analyses of prison conditions. The administration and classification of prisoners changed dramatically during this time. Haynes (1948) recounted these innovations in the following noteworthy passage:

> The development of a great variety of tests for individuals and groups during and since World War I has made possible more exact studies of personalities and their social relations. These tests have formed the basis for the wiser use of classification in many correctional institutions. Individualization of treatment of prisoners has become a reality in place of a goal to be hoped for but rarely attained (p. 434).

Rehabilitation replaced redemption as the main goal of imprisonment during the twentieth century. The medical orientation of rehabilitation brought more trained professionals into the American prison system. In order to classify inmates, progressive correctional facilities retained psychologists and psychiatrists. Haynes suggested that these trained clinicians introduced a more objective dimension to the administration of prisons, and set the stage for social scientific research in correctional facilities.

Matthews (1999) recounts early sociological studies of imprisonment. He notes that sociologists were first concerned with the maintenance of order inside prison. Scholars were particularly interested in the control and management of large numbers of prisoners with a minimal custodial presence. This concern intensified when bureaucratic administrations replaced authoritarian styles of management in prisons during the first part of the twentieth century. Matthews (1999) remarks that "this process of opening up the prison and providing more flexible, and in many cases, more liberal, regimes was accomplished paradoxically by an increase in the number of riots and disturbances in prisons" (p. 52). Sociologists examined the administrative changes that were taking place in American prisons, as well as the changes in the prisoners who were entering the system. Scholars became especially interested in social relations inside prison (Haynes, 1948). In particular, sociologists attributed the disturbances that were occurring inside U.S. prisons to the genesis of an inmate subculture.

The study of the inmate sociocultural sub-system involved several themes. First, the majority of this research centered around subcultural formation, or the etiology of the inmate subculture. As Matthews (1999) notes "one of the dominant themes in the early sociologies of imprisonment was the relationship between the outside culture from which the prisoners were drawn and the prison subculture itself" (p. 54). Researchers developed theories of deprivation and importation in order to explain subcultural formation. That is, the prison culture was believed to develop from either internal frustrations indicative of prison life or external socialization experiences.

Prisonization, the process of socialization or enculturation into the prison subculture, was another important area of sociological inquiry. Sociologists predicted the antecedents of prisonization by relying upon the deprivation and importation models of subcultural formation. For example, according to deprivation theory, frustrations such as a lack of autonomy contributed to prisonization. However, from the importation model, the inmate subculture was simply an extension of the criminal subculture on the outside. Therefore, indicators of prisonization included features of prior outside socialization. Lastly, a third line of research examined the consequences of assimilation into the inmate subculture. Thus, early sociologists of imprisonment tended to focus on the etiology of the inmate subculture, the antecedents of prisonization, and the consequences of assimilation into prison culture.

Most inquiry on imprisonment prior to the twentieth century was biased by humanitarian, religious, and political ideologies. This chapter is a review of the sociological foundations of correctional research. In particular, the general theoretical framework that supports the prisonization hypothesis is examined. These *competing* sociological theories form the basis for the current project.

**The Theoretical Background of Early Studies in Corrections**

The first scientific studies of imprisonment were influenced by the dominant structural-functional paradigm of the early twentieth century. Structural functionalism developed as a result of the classic work of Emile Durkheim. Durkheim (1895/1964) insisted that sociologists should empirically study social facts outside the scope of individual behavior such as social systems, cultural norms, and values. Parsons (1937) contributed to the structural-functional paradigm when he reinterpreted Durkheim's seminal work on social structure. Parsons was also concerned with different action systems. He examined the distinct systems and also the intersystemic relationships between them. Thus, a main tenet of structural-functionalism involves its emphasis on the sociocultural system. Furthermore, the maintenance of an orderly system was of foremost concern to the structural functionalists of the early twentieth century. The primary mechanism of systemic maintenance was socialization.

Sociologists of the early twentieth century approached the study of imprisonment from a structural-functional orientation. They were particularly interested in how order was maintained in a sociocultural sub-system (i.e., a prison) with inadequately socialized individuals (i.e., prisoners). From the structural-functional perspective, the prisonization hypothesis was advanced in order to explain social equilibrium inside prison. Several ideas were integral to the prisonization hypothesis, including subcultural formation, socialization, and enculturation. Each of these general concepts will be reviewed subsequently. Although structural functionalism provides an adequate basis for analyzing prison life, another paradigm known as symbolic interactionism is also beneficial in understanding social relations inside prison. Whereas structural functionalism dealt with social and cultural systems, symbolic interactionism focused on the social processes (e.g., socialization, development of self-concept, etc.) that individuals experience in society.

In fact, elements from both structural functionalism and symbolic interactionism form a theoretical basis for this study. The current project uses a mixed theoretical model in order to explain key social events that occur inside prison. The structural-functionalist orientation is well suited for multilevel analysis since it is truly a hierarchical theory that attempts to illustrate the interactions between individuals and sociocultural systems. It explains the origination of the inmate subculture. Symbolic interactionism tends to focus on individual-level mechanisms without reference to societal systems. Theories rooted in symbolic interactionism explain how inmates learn the norms of the inmate subculture and how these interactions influence their self-concepts and behaviors accordingly.

Two somewhat juxtaposed sociological paradigms form a theoretical basis for the current work. An integration of structural functionalism and symbolic interactionism is not prosposed. That endeavor is well beyond the scope of this exercise. In fact, the basic philosophical principles that underlie each paradigm may be too inconsistent to resolve. Kornhauser (1978) suggested that structural-functional theories of delinquency (e.g., strain theory) tend to support the contention that human nature is oriented toward conformist, prosocial behavior. However, theories of delinquency that are based on symbolic interactionist concepts (e.g., differential association, labeling theory, etc.) seem to imply that human nature is a blank slate which is influenced through a process of interaction with generalized others.

In addition to these fundamental philosophical differences, the two paradigms diverge on several other key concepts. The first of these is the rather pragmatic issue of an analytic level. Structural functionalism generally takes the social or cultural system as its level of analysis. Symbolic interactionism focuses on the individual. Of course, the current project examines both levels of analysis simultaneously. As such, this difference between the two paradigms is not very problematic. A more troublesome discrepancy between structural-functionalism and symbolic interactionism involves the notion of consensus versus conflict in society. According to structural functionalism, society is geared toward consensus. Symbolic interactionism makes no such claims about society. In fact, some symbolic interactionists see individuals in a constant state of conflict over scarce goods and resources in society.

Merton (1968) argued that three prevailing postulates in functional analysis caused considerable misunderstandings of the structural-functional paradigm. He actually suggested that these postulates in functional analysis may actually be unnecessary to the functional orientation. Merton (1968) specifies this holy trinity as follows:

> These postulates hold first, that standardized social activities or cultural items are functional for the *entire* social or cultural system, that *all* such social and cultural items fulfill sociological functions; and third, that these items are consequently *indispensable* (p. 79).

In critiquing these postulates, Merton made several valid points. First, he noted that cultural norms and customs have multiple consequences, including some that are functional and others that are dysfunctional. Ultimately, it depends upon the specification of the social unit in question whether cultural items do or do not serve a function. Merton also implied that consensus in society is not absolute. Rather, theorists must assess the net balances of functional consequences. Over time, certain sub-systems will arise that challenge the dominant sociocultural system. However, unless the counterculture completely overturns the dominant system (e.g., as in the case of revolutions), conventional order is still maintained. For instance, the inmate subculture generally is in conflict with and opposed to the custodial authority of the institution. Yet, order is usually maintained net the conflicts that occasionally arise between the inmate subculture and the dominant system (i.e., custodians). In sum, these concessions about consensus make the theoretical combination of structural functionalism and symbolic interactionism less problematic in the current project.

**The Phenomenon of Subcultural Formation**

Subcultural theory emerged as an effort to explain deviant social groups (e.g., see Shaw, 1931; Sutherland, 1937; Thrasher, 1927). The application of subcultural theory to the study of prison life was a natural progression in sociological thought. Matthews (1999) remarks that "this form of enquiry paralleled the development of subcultural theory within criminology and the growing number of studies which analysed how subcultures arise in response to collectively experienced problems and situations" (p. 54). The theory of subcultural formation as a functional solution to collectively experienced problems was also embedded within twentieth century structural functionalism.

Despite the fact that subcultural theory was initially entrenched within a single paradigm, there are still several definitions for the concept of a subculture. As such, it is necessary to consider the work of several different scholars when defining the concept of a subculture. Gordon (1947/1997) defined a subculture as follows:

> a sub-division of a national culture, composed of a combination of factorable social situations such as class status, ethnic background, regional and rural or urban residence, and religious affiliation, but *forming in their combination a functioning unity which has an integrated impact on the participating individual* (p. 41).

Yet, as Irwin (1970/1997) has pointed out, the grouping of individuals by race or place seems somewhat arbitrary. In fact, it is not clear how Gordon's cultural units relate to one another or other subsystems. Furthermore, Irwin also suggested that other members of the Chicago School simply conceptualized a subculture as any small group. Again, this definition seems rather arbitrary and pragmatic. Irwin offered a more theoretically grounded specification of the term. Irwin (1970/1997) contended that a subculture is actually quite similar to a reference group.

Shibutani (1956) conceptualized three different uses of the reference group concept. He wrote that "an examination of current usage discloses three distinct referents for a single concept: (1) groups which serve as comparison points; (2) groups to which men aspire; and (3) groups whose perspectives are assumed by the actor (Shibutani, 1956, p. 562). Shibutani (1956) suggested that individuals may also simultaneously belong to several different reference groups. For instance, he remarked that "in our mass society, characterized as it is by cultural pluralism, each person internalizes several perspectives" (Shibutani, 1956, p. 565). Irwin (1970/1997) extended Shibutani's (1956) reference group theory to encompass the definition of a subculture.

Subcultures are references groups of a particular sort. Irwin (1970/1997) offered the following specification:

> Subculture, rather than the subset of behavior patterns of a segment, or the patterns of a small group, is often thought of as a social world, a shared perspective, which is not attached firmly to any definite group or segment (p. 67).

Yet, there is one primary difference between Shibutani's (1956) work on reference groups and Irwin's (1970/1997) definition of a subculture. This difference concerns the extent to which involvement in subcultures or reference groups affects one's core self-concept. Shibutani (1956) predicted that reference group identification is essential to the development of one's self-concept. In fact, he believed that the internationalization of ideas associated with particular reference groups permanently alters one's self-concept. However, Irwin (1970/1997) was reluctant to accept this deterministic element of Shibutani's theory. Instead, he minimized the influence of subcultural identification on self-concept formation and change in order to preserve human agency and volunteerism. In sum, Irwin incorporated Shibutani's (1956) work on shared group perspectives in his definition of subculture but rejected the notion that subcultural involvement permanently alters one's core self-concept.

Irwin (1970/1997) also included folk metaphors in his specification of a subculture. In particular, he interpreted certain lifestyles and scenes as subcultures. In order for a lifestyle or scene to be a subculture, Irwin (1970/1997) suggested that it should meet the following three conditions:

> (1) The style of life is recognized as an explicit and shared category. In other words a particular scene is well known among some relatively large segment. It must be to be a scene, since the term connotes popularity. (2) There are various styles of life available to a particular person, since there is always more than one scene. (3) Finally, one's commitment to a particular scene is potentially tentative and variable (pp. 67-68).

Thus, since commitment to a lifestyle or scene is sometimes tentative, these types of subcultural organizations may have only transitory effects on human behavior. Again, Irwin (1970/1997) preserves volunteerism while providing a cultural account of human action.

Although structural-functionalists proposed several different definitions for the sociocultural sub-system known as a subculture, they appeared united in their explanation of subcultural formation. Cohen (1955/1997) articulated a general theory of subcultures during his investigation of delinquency among boys. The first assumption of his subcultural theory is that all human action is oriented toward solving problems. Problems involve some type of tension, disequilibrium, challenge, or conflict. Cohen (1955/1997) noted that problems originate from either circumstances associated with external situations or factors related to internal perspectives (i.e., frames of reference).

In particular, situational forces often create problems for individuals by limiting the options and opportunities available to them. Cohen (1955/1997) described a situation as including "the world we live in ... the physical setting within which we must operate, a finite supply of time and energy with which to accomplish our ends, and above all the habits, the expectations, the demands and the social organization of the people around us" (p. 45). He also noted that situational problems are relative. That is, actors confront situations with different interests, preconceptions, stereotypes, and values. Cohen seems to be discussing an *interaction* between macro, situational problems and micro, coping abilities. However, he never fully develops this thesis in his work.

Instead, Cohen (1955/1997) theorized that problems associated with an actor's frame of reference are paramount to situational problems. Problems related to one's perspective manifest as tension, frustration, resentment, guilt, bitterness, anxiety, and hopelessness. He focused on solutions directed at the individual rather than the situation or context. Cohen (1955/1997) made the following important observation:

> An effective, really satisfying solution *must entail some change in that frame of reference itself.* The actor must give up pursuit of some goal which seems unattainable, but is not a "solution" unless he can first persuade himself that the goal is, after all, not worth pursuing; in short, his values must change (p. 45).

Since many forms of situational problems are beyond individual control, changing one's perspective is the only alternative. Cohen mentioned that individuals develop different mechanisms of adjustment such as projection, rationalization, substitution, and reaction formation.

However, both the problems and solutions of modern life are disproportionately distributed along class boundaries. Cohen (1955/1997) suggested that "opportunities for achievement of power and prestige are not the same for people who start out at different positions in the class system" (p. 46). To some extent, social structure determines what options are available to confront and resolve life's problems. Cohen (1955/1997) went on to say that "the structure of society generates, at each position within the system, characteristic combinations of personality and situation and therefore characteristic problems of adjustment" (p. 46). Again, it appears as if Cohen was formulating a *multilevel* theory of subcultural formation. However, he considered situation as a constant force to which individuals orient themselves. Cohen only examined how several individuals deal differently with the same problem.

Nevertheless, a critical component of Cohen's (1955/1997) general theory of subcultures is that all human action is an effort to solve problems. In keeping with the structural-functional framework, the second main assumption of this general theory involves the notion that all human action is also oriented toward conformity to some group. That is, humans are social beings who are dependent upon each other within the broader social milieu. Cohen (1955/1997) argued that "not only is consensus rewarded by acceptance, recognition and respect; it is probably the most important criterion of the *validity* of the frame of reference which motivates and justifies our conduct" (p. 47). Individual perspectives are shaped by membership within specific reference groups.

In fact, some social groups are more effective at guiding individuals through the resolution of life's problems than others. Cohen (1955/1997) made the following important comment:

> Should our problems be not capable of solution in ways acceptable to our groups and should they be sufficiently pressing, we are not so likely to strike out on our own as we are to shop around for a group with a different subculture, with a frame of reference we find more congenial (p. 48).

In fact, Cohen theorized that individuals resolve their problems of adjustment by migrating between groups. This pattern of migration causes a continual realignment of groups in society. However, there may be instances when no group with a cultural model appropriate for solving the problems of certain individuals exists. If this is the case, then a new type of collective solution (i.e., subculture) may arise.

Interaction is essential to subcultural formation. Cohen (1955/1997) suggested that "the crucial condition for the emergence of new cultural forms is the existence, *in effective interaction with one another, of a number of actors with similar problems of adjustment*"(p. 48). This interaction must be mutual and anticipatory. That is, the formation of a subculture is dependent upon the joint and somewhat simultaneous efforts of individuals. Cohen (1955/1997) noted that

> For the actor with problems of adjustment which cannot be resolved within the frame of reference of the established culture, each response of the other to what the actor says and does is a clue to the directions in which change may proceed further in a way congenial to the other and to the direction in which change will lace social support (p. 49).

The subculture emerges in response to the needs of individuals who share similar problems. However, it is born of a collective. No one individual can accept responsibility for this new form of social organization. It involves a mutual conversion of all involved to a new frame of reference.

Cohen (1955/1997) concluded that "the emergence of these 'group standards' of this shared frame of reference, is the emergence of a new subculture" (p. 51). The normative system that comprises a subculture is shared among those with problems that stand to be resolved by the new models of action that become validated by the subculture. Additionally, Cohen noted that a subcultural system may only outlive the groups of individuals who participated in its creation as long as it offers solutions to the problems of those who follow its creators. In this sense, the entire existence and perpetuation of subcultures is functional.

**The Individual and the Sociocultural System**

The relationship between individual behavior and sociocultural order is reciprocal. Individuals impact the sociocultural system as they interact with one another. House (1992) remarked that "people are active agents who process inputs from their social environments and respond in ways that are not totally predictable and that may modify the effects of the environment and even the nature of the environment itself" (p. 555). As previously mentioned, individuals with adjustment problems may interact with one another in order to change the status quo or create a sociocultural sub-system (i.e., subculture) that more directly addresses their problems. Although a subculture is an expression of the collective needs of maladjusted individuals, it also impacts their subsequent beliefs and behaviors. The shared frame of reference becomes a normative system that directs future behavior. New cohorts must also learn the norms of the subculture and become socialized in subcultural ways.

In fact, the manner in which both culture and social structure affect individual behavior has been an important topic within the discipline of sociology. How an individual can be both a cause and a consequence of society has been a vexing question since the inception of the sociological enterprise (Allport, 1968). Nonetheless, cultural explanations of human behavior were popular during the first half of the twentieth century. From this perspective, adult behavior is a cultural product that results from the interactions in which humans engage. Environmental, structural, and cultural forces shape these interactions into specific patterns of socialization. Akers (1998) has suggested the following:

> The general culture and structure of society and the particular communities, groups, and other contexts of social interaction provide learning environments in which the norms define what is approved and disapproved, behavioral models are present, and the reactions of other people (for example, in applying social sanctions) and the existence of other stimuli attach different reinforcing or punishing consequences to individuals' behavior (p.322).

The process of socialization, in turn, influences adult personality and behavior (House, 1992). Socialization, or social learning, is the primary micro-processual mechanism that links the sociocultural system to individual behavior.

## The Process of Socialization

The concept of socialization is perhaps sociology's central notion. However, Gecas (1992) suggested that this process actually has two distinct meanings within the discipline. According to the structural-functional paradigm, socialization refers to an individual's adaption or conformity to the norms and values of a society. Socialization is the means by which a sociocultural system is perpetuated. Another sociological tradition, known as symbolic interactionism, focuses on the individual and tends to de-emphasize the sociocultural system. From this perspective, socialization is a process of personal development that an individual undergoes in response to social forces. Rather than focusing on cultural transmission, symbolic interactionists conceptualize socialization in terms of the development of self-concept and identity. In addition to the aforementioned discussion of consensus versus conflict in society, another difference between the structural-functional meaning of socialization and the symbolic interactionist version involves the level of analysis. Structural functionalists emphasize how integral socialization is to the maintenance of the sociocultural system; symbolic interactionists stress how crucial socialization is to the development of the individual. Both meanings of socialization are germane since the current project involves both the micro and the macro levels of analysis.

Definitions of socialization range from those very specific in nature to others that are quite general. It is the more general definitions that are of interest here. Sewell (1963) defines socialization as "the processes by which individuals selectively acquire skills, knowledge, attitudes, values, and motives in current groups of which they are or will become members" (p. 163). This definition illustrates the positive effects of socialization for both the individual and the sociocultural system.

Anthropologists have advanced a notion similar to socialization. Herskovits (1949) coined the term *enculturation* to refer to "the process of conscious or unconscious conditioning, exercised within the limits sanctioned by a given body of custom" (p. 39). Sociocultural learning begins in infancy and ends with death. Indeed, the most important phase of enculturation occurs during childhood. Herskovits (1949) suggested that "the enculturation of the individual in the early years of his life is the prime mechanism making for cultural stability, while the process as it is operative on more mature folk, is highly important in inducing change" (p. 40). The learning experiences of later life are intermittent in that they do not cover as many aspects of culture. Herskovits (1949) made the following insight:

> The adult knows his language, the systems of etiquette that regulate behavior, how to face the supernatural, the musical forms of his culture - all the things that the child must learn. For the adult, enculturation has been completed *except* where new situations must be met, new choices made; his culture, in the main, has been learned so well that he need give it little thought (p. 41).

The process of enculturation is necessary in order for an individual to become a member of society. It exerts a powerful force during the early years, but still influences individuals later in life. Enculturation occurs over the life course and is beneficial as a means of cultural transmission as well as individual development.

Socialization and enculturation share much conceptual similarity. The idea of intermittent enculturation is similar to what Berger and Berger (1972) have termed secondary socialization. Secondary socialization includes the later processes that individuals experience when they are induced into a particular social world. Primary socialization, on the other hand, involves the initial processes whereby a child becomes a attendant member of a sociocultural system. The extent to which primary and secondary socialization processes are similar has been an area of considerable debate among sociologists (Clausen, 1968; Sewell, 1963). Yet, according to Bush and Simmons (1992), "it appears that differences between them involve the content and context of socialization more than actual processual differences" (p. 136). They go on to say that adult socialization is more likely to include role-learning and self-initiated socialization, whereas imitation and identification may be more indicative of childhood socialization.

Secondary socialization is also likely to occur within a specific situation. Becker (1964) suggests that personal change in adult life is related to situational adjustment. Situational adjustment is similar to the concept of intermittent enculturation. Becker (1964) describes the process of situational adjustment as follows:

> The person, as he moves in and out of a variety of social situations, learns the requirements of continuing in each situation and of success in it. If he has a strong desire to continue, the ability to assess accurately what is required, and can deliver the required performance, the individual turns himself into the kind of person the situation demands (p. 44).

The concept of situational adjustment is actually a social structural explanation of personal change. As Becker (1964) notes "the structural characteristics of institutions and organizations provide the framework of the situations in which experience dictates the expediency of change" (p. 52). Thus, sociocultural sub-systems provide the contexts of socialization and change in adulthood.

Kennedy and Kerber (1973) have suggested that primary socialization is accomplished through several key mechanisms. They first discussed the importance of nonverbal responses as a prerequisite for the acquisition of language. Nonverbal communication is particularly important for primary socialization during infancy because these cues relay feelings in the absence of speech. Next, Kennedy and Kerber examined both the meaning of and the acquisition of language. They suggested that "language and its symbols make possible ideas and communication of ideas" (Kennedy & Kerber, 1973, p. 6). Kennedy and Kerber maintained that the meaning of language is learned by a process of conditioning. That is, the transformation of actual behavior into ideas occurs through a process of stimulus-response, instrumental learning, positive reinforcement, and punishment. The acquisition of language enables individuals to plan, evaluate, and convey meaning. In short, language permits individuals to think.

Kennedy and Kerber (1973) also emphasized the influence of primary groups on the socialization process. Primary groups include the family, the playgroup, and the neighborhood community group. According to Kennedy and Kerber (1973), "the primary group is responsible for the initial inculcation of language and perceptions" (p. 11). In the context of these primary groups, an individual's sense of the looking-glass self (e.g., see Cooley, 1964) and the generalized other (e.g., see Mead, 1964) are developed. This enables the individual to see himself as others do, and incorporate external expectations into his own self-concept. These groups are especially important during primary socialization.

However, as Bush and Simmons (1992) have noted, self-initiated socialization and role learning may be more characteristic of secondary socialization. Self-socialization occurs when individuals begin to break away from primary groups, particularly peer groups, and begin to form their own judgments concerning their behavior. During self-initiated socialization, an individual sets goals that are consistent with a particular reference group and begins to act in a manner appropriate to attain these goals. Kennedy and Kerber (1973) defined this anticipatory socialization as "a process by which the individual prepares himself for acceptance into a group in terms of its required values, abilities, and roles" (p. 17). In fact, the process of role learning begins with anticipatory socialization (Thornton & Nardi, 1975).

Since modern society is so complex, differentiated, and rapidly changing, role learning is a distinct facet of adult socialization. Bush and Simmons (1992) remarked that "individuals simply cannot be prepared in childhood for all the tasks and roles they will encounter as adults" (p. 144). In fact, social roles are constantly changing and new roles continuously emerge. Bush and Simmons also have noted that role learning also involves role transitions and discontinuities. They suggested that role discontinuity (i.e., a difference in the demands of a new and an old role) may be a psychologically stressful processes. Several factors intensify discontinuity and, thereby, increase stress. Both inadequate preparation for a new role and any loss of status associated with it compound role discontinuity. Bush and Simmons (1992) also suggested that "if such role transitions occur earlier or later in life than prescribed by the norms, then stress associated with them will be exacerbated, and socialization to the new role may be faulty or incomplete" (p. 148).

Furthermore, individuals may experience discontinuity when there is either a lack of role clarity or increased conflict between roles and statuses. In sum, adult socialization may be interrupted by a variety of factors associated with the stress that accompanies role learning.

## Resocialization

Individuals become functioning members of society through socialization. During this process, individuals learn how to communicate, live according to society's rules and norms, and obtain sustenance. However, as Kennedy and Kerber (1973) have proposed, socialization sometimes fails. They suggested that "an individual is considered to be poorly socialized by the dominant society when his behavior does not comply with its norms" (p. 29). In fact, there are visible failures in the educational, criminolegal, and industrial institutions. Illiterates, high school dropouts, criminals, the unemployed, those on welfare, and lifelong dependents are all examples of individuals with inadequate socialization.

Resocialization is a process that may correct inadequate social learning and restore broader social consonance. In particular, Kennedy and Kerber (1973) advanced programs of resocialization in three major social institutions (i.e., education, criminal justice, and industry). They defined resocialization in the following manner:

> Resocialization is that process wherein an individual, defined as inadequate according to the norms of a dominant institution(s), is subjected to a dynamic program of behavior intervention aimed at instilling and/or rejuvenating those values, attitudes, and abilities which would allow him to function according to the norms of said dominant institution(s) (Kennedy and Kerber, 1973, p. 39).

Criminal rehabilitation is the primary resocialization procedure associated with the justice system. According to Kennedy and Kerber (1972), rehabilitation involves a process whereby "an individual is, theoretically, exposed to a set of conditions which lead him to realize that behavior conforming to the dominant norms brings more emotional and material rewards than behavior opposing the dominant norms" (p. 42). The logic of rehabilitation seems sound. However, a more detailed examination of the context of socialization in prison illustrates a potential problem.

Gecas (1992) has remarked that "*all* socialization is contextual in that it occurs in some social situation" (p. 167). Prison is one such context in which secondary socialization may occur. Advocates of resocialization have promoted incarceration as an opportunity to rehabilitate or correct a deviant's internalization of the rules and norms of the dominant sociocultural system (Wheeler, 1966). However, Cohen's (1955/1997) work on subcultures supports an alternative consequence of incarceration. Subcultures arise when individuals with similar adjustment problems (i.e., inadequate socialization) begin interacting with one another. When similar individuals are grouped together during incarceration, an inmate subculture may emerge as an unintended consequence of imprisonment. It is possible that the emergence of an inmate subculture undermines the very objectives of resocialization and rehabilitation.

**The Sociological Investigation of Prison Life**

The scientific inquiry of prison life began in the early twentieth century. Sociologists initially approached this field of study from a structural-functional orientation. Structural functionalism emphasizes the relationship of social structure to individual behavior. Scholars of imprisonment were initially interested in social order and control inside the institution. Meanwhile, theories of subcultural formation and socialization also emerged from the structural-functional paradigm. Subcultures are sociocultural sub-systems that function to maintain social consonance. They arise as a collective solution to the problems of a group of individuals with similar difficulties. Socialization functions to perpetuate the sociocultural order. Yet according to an alternative sociological perspective (i.e., symbolic interactionism), socialization is integral to the development of the self. Specifically, primary and secondary socialization occur at different points throughout life. Both imply enculturation. However, secondary socialization is more intermittent and often involves situational adjustment. While the paradigms of symbolic interactionism and structural functionalism are based on competing underlying assumptions, they form the theoretical basis for the current project. In fact, this research implies a mixed theoretical model.

The purpose of this chapter has been to detail the sociological foundations for correctional research. In particular, interest in penology evolved during the twentieth century as it became somewhat more academic and scientific than previous endeavors. Also, early scholars of imprisonment were initially writing from a distinct structural functional theoretical orientation. The current project deviates from that perspective by incorporating elements from symbolic interactionism.

# CHAPTER 3
# Life Inside Prison

Scientific inquiry on imprisonment commenced during the first half of the twentieth century. Pollock (1997) has divided extant scholarship on life inside prison into two broad historical categories. Researchers examined the social processes associated with the inmate subculture during the first phase of this investigation. Pollock (1997) maintains that "between the 1940s and 1960s prison researchers were concerned with the definition of, and socialization to, the prisoner subculture" (p. 246). Sociologists during this time frame developed theories that explained the origin of the inmate subculture. They also explored the mechanism of socialization into this sociocultural sub-system and termed it prisonization. Their classical work on life inside prison was primarily centered around three concepts: the prisoner subculture, the inmate code, and prisonization.

However, these substantive areas were replaced by other topics during the second phase of prison research. Pollock (1997) suggests that "even as researchers were utilizing various research modalities to study the prison world, it was changing rapidly and inevitably in response to events both outside and inside the prison walls" (p. 246). She attributes change in correctional research agendas to several historical incidents, such as the general unrest of the 1960s, the black awareness movement, and increased racial minorities, gangs, and drugs in prison. Whatever the cause, contemporary scholarship on imprisonment from 1960 to 1990 has focused on a variety of issues including prison crowding and prison gangs.

In this project, Pollock's (1997) general differentiation between classical correctional research (i.e., referring to roughly the first two-thirds of the past century) and contemporary scholarship (i.e., referring to the last third of the twentieth century) is maintained. In this sense, the current project is grounded in classical research on imprisonment where the goal is to determine if traces of the inmate subculture persist in modern correctional facilities. Also of interest is the process of secondary socialization or intermittent enculturation, known as prisonization, that inmates undergo once inside prison. Although classical lines of research are primarily re-examined in the present study, contemporary elements are also included. Contemporary constructs such as gang involvement may be related to prisonization. The background for the current project is drawn from both phases of correctional research.

Specifically, extant work on the inmate subculture is examined. The three aforementioned, sociological areas of investigation (i.e., the etiology of inmate subculture, the antecedents of prisonization, and the consequences of prisonization) are reviewed more thoroughly. Both the deprivation and importation models of subcultural formation are discussed, and an integration of these competing theories is suggested. The micro and macro antecedents of prisonization are also specified. Finally, aspects of modern correctional facilities, such as overcrowding and prison gangs, that are relevant to a modern understanding of prisonization are explored.

## The Big House

All research on imprisonment must be interpreted in terms of the context in which it occurred. According to Irwin (1980), classical research on prison life took place inside the Big House. Irwin (1980) made the following insightful observation:

> The Big House was the source of images and illusions that continue to obscure the contemporary prison. Some of these images and illusions were created by sociologists who began investigating the prison in the 1930s and have since become the authorities on life there (p. 29).

The Big House is an archetype that, as Irwin (1980) put it, "has been the source of most of our ideas about prisons" (p. 3). It is within this context that most scientific inquiry on imprisonment began.

Irwin (1980) offers a vivid account of the physical description of the Big House:

> The Big House was a walled prison with large cell blocks that contained stacks of three or more tiers of one- or two-man cells.

On average, it held 2,500 men. Sometimes a single cell block housed over 1,000 prisoners in six tiers of cells (p. 3).

The cells were described as conforming to these standards:

> Their cells had toilets and small sinks, and they were ventilated, heated, clean, and slightly more spacious. In many Big Houses, convicts were permitted to add furnishings, and decorations to their cells, and many cells had rugs on the floor, paintings on the walls, and other pieces of furniture that fit into the small space between the bunks of the cell wall (Irwin, 1980, p. 4).

Other distinguishing features of the Big House included its recreation yard, the mess hall, the administration building, the shops, and the industries. Irwin (1980) summed up his description of the Big House as a "granite, steel, cement, and asphalt monstrosity" (p. 5).

Life inside the Big House involved isolation and monotony. Irwin (1980) described the routine of prison life as follows:

> Prisoners rose early; hurriedly ate breakfast; returned to their cells for one of the four or five daily counts; proceeded to work, school, or the yard for a day of idleness; hurriedly ate lunch; counted; went back to work, school, or idleness; hurriedly ate dinner; and returned to their cells for the night (p. 10).

This pattern was the mainstay of life in the Big House. However, other social elements punctuated the monotony. At night, the inmates would write letters, pursue hobbies, talk to each other, and listen to the radio. During the weekends, sporting events (i.e., baseball games and sanctioned boxing) and visits alleviated some of the monotony. In sum, the Big House was a context that exerted its influence upon both the inmates doing time there and the sociologists who studied them.

**Prisons as Total Institutions**

The Big House was a total institution. According to Goffman (1961), a total institution has a character "symbolized by the barrier to social intercourse with the outside and to departure that is often built right into the physical plant, such as locked doors, high walls, barbed wire, cliffs, water, forests, or moors" (p. 4). Other examples of total institutions include mental hospitals, orphanages, boarding schools, merchant ships, army barracks, monasteries, convents, and retirement homes. The element common to these institutions is the handling of human needs by the bureaucratic organization en masse. They are part formal organization and part residential community. Total institutions are social hybrids.

Goffman (1961) used the method of the ideal type to discern characteristics common to total institutions. He enumerated four general qualities of total institutions. Goffman (1961) listed these as follows:

> First, all aspects of life are conducted in the same place and under the same single authority. Second, each phase of the member's daily activity is carried on in the immediate company of a large batch of others, all of whom are treated alike and required to do the same thing together. Third, all phases of the day's activities are tightly scheduled, with one activity leading at a prearranged time into the next, the whole sequence of activities being imposed from above by a system of explicit formal rulings and a body of officials. Finally, the various enforced activities are brought together into a single rational plan purportedly designed to fulfill the official aims of the institution (p. 6).

These characteristics are not common to any one type of total institution. Instead, these qualities vary in the extent to which they apply to the different institutional forms.

Two main social groups are found in total institutions. Goffman (1961) maintained that "in total institutions there is a basic split between a large managed group, conveniently called inmates, and a small supervisory staff" (p. 7). Inmates spend their daily lives inside the institutions while staff work there and remain part of the conventional sociocultural order. Goffman (1961) further remarked that "social mobility between the two strata is grossly restricted; social distance is typically great and often formally prescribed" (p. 7). Thus, the barriers within total institutions are both physical and social. The social world in which inmates live reflects these ever-present barriers and tensions.

The inmate world involves a distinct social organization that is at odds with sociocultural sub-systems on the outside. Goffman (1961) made the following insightful comment:

> Total institutions do not substitute their own unique culture for something already formed... They create and maintain a particular kind of tension between the home world and the institutional world and use this persistent tension as strategic leverage in the management of men (p. 13).

Total institutions are juxtaposed against conventional society and function as constant reminders of the relations and luxuries that inmates are denied inside prison. In this sense, the inmate subculture stands independent of the dominant sociocultural order.

## The Inmate Subculture

The inmate subculture is a unique, subterranean social order inside prison. Clemmer (1958) observed that the particular elements of this special sociocultural sub-system include the following:

> habits, behavior systems, traditions, history, customs, folkways, codes, the laws and rules which guide the inmates and their ideas, opinions and attitudes toward or against homos, family, education, work, recreations, government, prisons, police, judges, other inmates, wardens, ministers, doctors, guards, ballplayers, clubs, guns, cells, buckets, gravy, beans, walls, lamps, rain, clouds, clothes, machinery, hammers, rocks, caps, bibles, books, radios, monies, stealing, murder, rape, sex, love, honesty, martyrdom, and so on (pp. 294-295).

The inmate subculture involves a system of power and interchange, albeit illegitimate, that includes specific normative expectations, values, and behavioral outcomes.

The inmate code forms the basis for the normative system of this prisoner subculture. Ohlin (1956) offered a particularly insightful description of the inmate code as follows:

> The [inmate] code represents an organization of criminal values in clearcut opposition to the values of conventional society, and to prison officials as representatives of that society. The main tenet of this code forbids any type of supportive or nonexploitative liaison with prison officials. It seeks to confer status and prestige on those inmates who stand most clearly in opposition to the administration (p. 28).

Pollock (1997) has called it the *Magna Carta* of the prisoner sociocultural sub-system.

The inmate code also forms the basis for the values and behaviors that are indicative of the prisoner subculture. Wilder (1965) has noted that the primary values of the convict subculture were group loyalty, violence, strength, and sexual proclivity. Ohlin (1956) described these values and beliefs as follows:

> These criminal beliefs and attitudes place a high premium on physical violence and strength, on exploitative sex relations, and predatory attitudes toward money and property. They place a strong emphasis on in-group loyalty and solidarity and on aggressive and exploitative relations with conventionally oriented out-groups (p. 29).

Of course, not every prisoner is actively involved in the inmate subculture. However, most are aware of the inmate code and respect it. This normative system develops from the perspectives of individuals who share similar problems of adjustment.

Sociocultural sub-systems arise when a number of inadequately socialized individuals with similar adjustment problems interact with one another (Cohen, 1955/1997). Irwin and Cressey (1962) observed that "we have no doubt that the total set of relationships called 'inmate society' is a response to problems of imprisonment" (p. 145). However, as Thomas (1971) pointed out, scholars have been divided as to the exact factors that contribute to the origination of the convict subculture. Two distinct models have been advanced in scientific discourse.

## The Deprivation Model

According to one popular perspective, known as the deprivation model or indigenous influence theory, the inmate subculture emerged as a direct result of the adjustment problems that are particular to life inside prison. That is, the subculture arose in order to compensate for the deprivations of prison life. Sykes (1958) is typically credited with the most complete articulation of this perspective. He coined the phrase, *pains of imprisonment*, to describe the harsh reality of the New Jersey State Prison. According to Sykes (1958), the pains of imprisonment include the following:

> The deprivations or frustrations of prison life today ... viewed as punishments which the free community deliberately inflicts on the offender for violating the law ... that can be just as painful as the physical maltreatment ... [and] appear as a serious attack on the personality, as a threat to the life goals of the individual, to his defensive system, to the self-esteem, or to his feelings of security (p. 64).

He continued to enumerate these unpleasantries as the deprivation of liberty, the deprivation of goods and services, the deprivation of heterosexual relations, the deprivation of autonomy, and the deprivation of security. Sykes charged that inmates perceive the deprivations and frustrations of prison life as painful *in the extreme*. He also suggested that this perception was uniform among prisoners.

In sum, the deprivation model proposes that a variety of pains, stresses, and problems associated with imprisonment and the criminal justice system in general labels inmates and thus confronts them with problems of adjustment that require a collective, subcultural response. Thomas and Petersen (1977) described the processes that occur after the initial formation of the inmate subculture:

> Once such a [subcultural] response occurs, an inmate society
> begins to take form, a society that includes a network of positions
> which reflect various types and levels of subcultural norms as
> well as adaptive reactions to the problems of confinement, a
> system of rewards and sanctions that encourage compliance to
> the normative expectations associated with these positions, and
> a socialization process which is directed toward the goal of
> increasing the level of appreciation for and responsiveness to the
> prescriptions and proscriptions of the inmate code (p. 49).

The entire machinery of the inmate subculture is an attempt to alleviate
deprivations.

## The Importation Model

Another well-known perspective, known as the importation model or
cultural drift theory, proposed that the inmate subculture was a product of
the latent, street culture to which most prisoners belonged prior to their
incarceration. In fact, Irwin (1980) suggested that the inmate code was
itself a prison adaptation of the thieves' code. He observed that thieves
were the most frequent criminal type imprisoned in the Big House. They
had a strong communication network which ensured that their values
would be imported from the outside and become permanent fixtures of the
inmate subculture. Their code dominated the correctional facilities of the
early twentieth century. Irwin (1980) made the following insightful
observation:

> The central rule in the thieves' code was 'thou shalt not snitch.'
> In prison, thieves converted this to the dual norm of 'do not rat
> on another prisoner' and 'do your own time.' Thieves were also
> obliged by their code to be cool and tough, that is to maintain
> respect and dignity; not to show weakness; to help other thieves;
> and to leave most other prisoners alone (p. 12).

The inmate code could easily be extrapolated from the thieves' code. Specifically, Irwin (1980) suggested that the thieves code translated into three tenets of the inmate code: do not inform, do not openly interact or cooperate with the guards or the administration, and do your own time.

Although the inmate subculture was comprised of a variety of prisoners, thieves established a dominant presence in it. In particular, Irwin and Cressey (1962) discussed the adaptation of the thieves to imprisonment in the following noteworthy passage:

> Imprisonment is one of the recurring problems with which thieves must cope. It is almost certain that a thief will be arrested from time to time, and the subculture provides members with patterns to be used in order to help them solve this problem (pp. 146-147).

Appropriate ways of dealing with imprisonment included remaining trustworthy and skilled as a con or thief.

Irwin and Cressey (1962) took a very different stance on the origin of the inmate subculture than did Sykes (1958). Instead of viewing the inmate subculture as arising to address the pains of imprisonment, Irwin and Cressey (1962) maintained that the inmate subculture was an institutionalized version of the outside, criminal subculture (i.e., particularly the outside thief subculture). In other words, they believed that the inmate subculture drifted inside prison from the outside. In their view, the inmate subculture did not originate in response to problems encountered inside prison. Rather, thieves and other inmates dealt with the problems of prison by relying upon norms and using skills obtained during their socialization in the outside, criminal subculture. Furthermore, it is important to note that Irwin and Cressey (1962) and Sykes (1958) were describing the same, dominant inmate subculture in prison. They simply disagreed as to its origin.

**Integration**

When scholars first began studying the inmate subculture, they proposed the deprivation model in order to account for the emergence of this unique sociocultural sub-system. Later, researchers developed the importation model as an alternative explanation for the origin of the inmate subculture. The importation model was pitted against the deprivation model in empirical analyses. Perhaps it is not surprising that neither theory was dominant in this contest. Rather than detract from each other, the theories seemed to actually complement one another (Thomas, 1971; Thomas & Petersen, 1977). In fact, Schwartz (1971) submitted that both theories are wrong when stated in terms that deny one another. Thomas and Petersen (1977) wrote that "the deprivation model identifies certain structural conditions that may be viewed as a sufficient condition for the emergence of *some type* of adaptive response, but that these conditions are not sufficient to predict the nature of the response" (p. 51). Involvement in the inmate subculture hinges on pre-prison socialization experiences. In other words, certain prisoners are at a higher risk for involvement in the convict subculture based on pre-prison characteristics. Consequently, both the deprivation and importation models have implications for the micro-sociological process of prisonization.

**Prisonization**

Clemmer (1940) was the first person to fully articulate the process of prisonization. He engaged in cultural studies where inmates were allowed a voice through their letters, biographies, and personal accounts. Clemmer was able to follow inmates throughout their time inside prison. His work provided a rich description of the social processes associated with incarceration. In regard to Clemmer's research, Irwin (1980) commented that "in spite of the shortcomings and in spite of the middle-class moral cast that dulls or distorts some of his analysis, it is still the most complete study of the prison" (p. 32). Through qualitative research, he was able to identify prisonization and detail the elements that he believed exacerbated and moderated the process.

Prisonization involves a process of assimilation or socialization that Clemmer (1958) described as "a slow, gradual, more or less unconscious process during which a person learns enough of the culture of a social unit into which he is placed to make him characteristic of it" (pp. 298-299). He fully defined prisonization as "the taking on in greater or less degree of the folkways, mores, customs, and general culture of the penitentiary" (Clemmer, 1958, p. 299). Prisonization is essentially secondary socialization inside correctional facilities whereby inmates undergo a process of enculturation into the inmate subculture that includes adoption of the inmate code in greater or less degree.

Furthermore, Clemmer (1950) specified the following seven universal features of prisonization:

> Acceptance of an inferior role, accumulation of facts concerning the organization of the prison, the development of somewhat new habits of eating, dressing, working, sleeping, the adoption of local language, the recognition that nothing is owed to the environment for the supplying of needs, and the eventual desire for a good job are aspects of prisonization which are operative for all inmates (p. 316).

The accumulation of facts concerning the organization of the prison includes learning the nuances of the inmate code. Clemmer (1940) also speculated that prisonization may actually disrupt the personalities of inmates and make their adjustment on the outside *next to impossible*. In fact, inmate informants corroborated that prisonization was the most detrimental factor affecting post-prison adjustment.

Prisonization involves both enculturation into the inmate subculture and a process of disculturation that strips inmates of prior identities. Goffman (1961) observed that

> If the inmate's stay is long, what has been called "disculturation" may occur - that is, an "untraining" which renders him temporarily incapable of managing certain features of daily life on the outside, if and when he gets back to it (p. 13).

Imprisonment strips an inmate of the supports of his home world. Goffman referred to this as the mortification of self.

The mortification of self begins with degradation ceremonies that inmates undergo when they first enter a total institution. This process involves the stripping away of one's name, usual appearance, possessions, identity, and sense of personal safety. Goffman (1961) described the loss of status associated with these initiations as follows:

Admission procedures and obedience tests may be elaborated into a form of initiation that has been called "the welcome," where staff or inmates, or both, go out of their way to give the recruit a clear notion of his plight. As part of this rite of passage he may be called by a term such as "fish" or "swab," which tells him that he is merely an inmate, and what is more, that he has a special low status even in this low group (p. 18).

Inmates in total institutions are humiliated and degraded to the point that their former perspectives are invaded by the prison environment and the inmate subculture. Thus, before enculturation into the inmate sociocultural sub-system can commence, inmates must be adequately stripped of the influences of the outside world. Moreover, those inmates who experience the greatest disculturation are quite likely to immerse themselves in the inmate subculture. Goffman (1961) maintained that disculturation and mortification were absolute social processes. However, these mechanisms of assimilation are most likely intermittent. That is, inmates are not completely stripped of the remnants of their home worlds (Irwin, 1980; Thomas & Petersen, 1977). Some identities remain intact, and prisonization occurs in varying degrees throughout the inmate population.

## Micro Antecedents of Prisonization

The micro antecedents of prisonization include the individual characteristics of inmates that affect socialization into the inmate subculture. Both pre-prison characteristics and situational deprivations influence the degree of prisonization into the convict subculture. Indigenous influence theory suggests that the situational deprivations of prison life determine the degree of prisonization. Cultural drift theory, on the other hand, proposes that pre-prison characteristics influence prisonization. Scholars agree that both the deprivation and importation models are relevant for understanding the micro antecedents of prisonization (Akers, Hayner, & Gruninger, 1977; Thomas, 1971; Thomas & Petersen, 1977). Prior research has enumerated several antecedents of prisonization that include variables from both theoretical models.

Classical scholars of imprisonment believed that the determinants of prisonization were related. Haynes (1948) enumerated the following list of interrelated antecedents:

Whether or not complete prisonization occurs depends on a number of determining factors. It depends: (1) on the man himself, his personality; (2) the kind and extent of relationships which he had outside; (3) his affiliations with prison groups; (4) chance placement in work gang, cellhouse, and with cellmate; (5) acceptance of the dogmas or codes of the prison culture.

He also noted that prisonization was related to sociodemographic characteristics such as age, criminality, nationality, race, and regional conditioning.

Clemmer (1940) discussed seven factors that influence the extent of prisonization. First, he noted that a higher degree of prisonization is typically associated with longer prison sentences. An unstable personality is also indicative of higher prisonization. Third, a high degree of prisonization is related to a lack of contact with individuals outside prison. The integration into primary groups in prison is also associated with a more prisonized inmates. Fifth, a higher degree of prisonization is also linked with a blind acceptance of the dogmas and mores of the primary prison group. Chance also affects prisonization; an inmate is more likely to be prisonized if he is placed with others of a similar orientation. Lastly, a higher degree of prisonization is associated with participation in gambling and abnormal sexual behavior. Clemmer believed that the opposite conditions result in less prisonization. For example, he noted that short sentences are related to a lesser degree of prisonization.

Prisonization seems to involve a temporal element. Wheeler (1961) examined the association of prisonization with time served, phase of incarceration, prior penal commitments, and primary prison group contacts. Wheeler was particularly interested in determining if prisonization was more related to time served or some phase of incarceration. He divided a stratified random sample of 237 subjects by their phase of incarceration and examined their conformity to custodial authority. Wheeler (1961) described three main phases:

a) those who have served less than six months in the correctional
community and are thus in an *early phase* of their commitment;
b) those who have less than six months remaining to serve - the
*late phase* inmates; and c) those who have served more than six
months and have more than six months left to serve - the *middle
phase* inmates (p. 706).

Specifically, he discovered a U-shaped relationship between the inmates'
institutional conformity and their phase of incarceration. That is, the length
of sentence was not linearly related to prisonization as first hypothesized
by Clemmer (1940); instead, inmates in earlier and later phases of
incarceration conformed more to custodial authority than did inmates who
were in the middle phase of incarceration.

Wheeler (1961) contributed to the specification of prisonization in
different ways as well. Most notably, he was responsible for quantifying
the concept of prisonization in a very unique manner. Wheeler
conceptualized the inmate code as a dual normative orientation comprised
of attitudes and beliefs that reflect both opposition to custodial staff and
loyalty to other inmates. He developed vignettes that assessed the moral
reasoning of inmates. Subjects were asked to agree or disagree with the
decisions reached by the protagonists in the vignettes. Wheeler's
quantitative survey methodology was significantly different from the
qualitative participant observation used by prior researchers (e.g., see
Clemmer, 1940; Haynes, 1948).

In fact, quantitative techniques allowed researchers to test the
universality of prisonization across correctional institutions. Clemmer
(1940) had portrayed Menard, the maximum-security prison in southern
Illinois where he conducted his research, as a universal type. That is,
Clemmer implied that all prisons were identical and that only the
individual characteristics of inmates should affect prisonization. Wheeler
(1961) commented that "current correctional systems increasingly depart
from this image, and it is likely that both type of clientele and institutional
program exert an effect on social processes" (p. 709). He was aware of the
changing nature of correctional institutions and the influence that they
exert on the process of prisonization.

Although Wheeler's (1961) work represents a sophistication of the concept of prisonization, attempts to replicate his findings have been mixed. Atchley and McCabe (1968) used a stratified random sample of 403 prisoners incarcerated in a federal facility. Yet, when they divided the sample by phase of incarceration and examined the degree of conformity to custodial authority, no relationship was observed. Atchley and McCabe (1968) were unable to duplicate the U-shaped distribution of prisonization that Wheeler (1961) had established. However, Atchley and McCabe (1968) noted that the effect of the phase of incarceration on prisonization could be mediated by some unknown third variable. In short, they found no statistically significant relationships between prisonization and a number of predictors such as time served, phase of incarceration, and frequency or intensity of contact among inmates.

However, other researchers reported results similar to Wheeler's (1961) findings. Wellford (1967) examined the temporal element of prisonization as well. He drew a random sample of 120 inmates from a correctional facility in the District of Columbia. Wellford compared the effects on prisonization of both time served and phase of incarceration. There was no significant relationship between the amount of time served and the degree of prisonization. However, Wellford did observe a weak but significant effect of phase of incarceration on prisonization. He also extended work on social types in prison and determined that the degree of prisonization was related to a criminal social type. In sum, Wellford's (1967) study provided some support for Wheeler's (1961) finding that an inmate's phase of incarceration was related to his degree of prisonization.

Many studies of prisonization in the 1960s also focused on the level of interpersonal ties between inmates. In fact, Clemmer (1940), Haynes (1948), and Wheeler (1961) proposed that the extent of primary group contacts inside prison is an important determinant of prisonization. However, Stratton (1967) found no significant association between prisonization and inside contacts. In fact, he observed that inmate loyalty and measures of primary prison group contacts were not significantly correlated. He even examined post-institutional friendships between inmates, but found no relationship between this measure of contact and prisonization.

Tittle and Tittle (1964) also specified additional situational antecedents of socialization into the inmate subculture. They interviewed subjects in a hospital for narcotic addicts. Tittle and Tittle examined several determinants of prisonization, including the length of time spent incarcerated, prior incarcerations, the difficulties of prison life, alienation, meaningful participation in therapy, and disparities between aspirations and expectations. They found that, as time served increased, so did prisonization. Previous incarcerations also enhanced the degree of prisonization. Incidentally, Tittle and Tittle (1964) reaffirmed that "the pains of imprisonment do decrease with greater integration into the prisoner social organization, as indicated by the subscription to the prison code" (p. 218). They also found that higher degrees of prisonization were positively associated with both feelings of alienation and disparities between aspirations and expectations.

Several early studies of prisonization also focused on the association of argot roles with the adoption of the inmate code. Sykes (1958) maintained that "the society of captives exhibits a number of distinctive tags for the distinctive social roles played by its members in response to the particular problems of imprisonment" (p. 86). Sykes also discussed how prisonization was related to the adoption of certain roles. Social roles were required for the inmate subculture to effectively function. He also discussed a number of different argot roles, including rats, center men, gorillas, merchants, wolves, punks, fags, ball busters, real men, toughs, and hipsters. However, only the role of the real man increased inmate solidarity and reduced the pains of imprisonment for the inmate population as a whole. Schrag (1961) also outlined a set of role adaptations that included the square john, right guy, con, politician, ding, and outlaw. Garabedian (1963) suggested that specific roles were strongly associated with prisonization. For example, he suggested that right guys and outlaws were the most prisonized role types while square johns and dings were the least prisonized. Thus, this unique line of research examined the relationship of the argot inmate roles of the inmate social system to the process of prisonization.

The concept of prisonization also seems to hold up cross-nationally. In their study of the Pentonville Prison in London, Morris and Morris (1962) suggested that the degree of prisonization was dependent upon the following factors:

1. The extent of previous exposure to prison culture, both in terms of the number and duration of sentences.
2. The nature of the relationship maintained with the outside.
3. The degree to which the prisoner consciously accepts the dogmas and codes of the inmate culture.
4. The nature of the prisoner's relationships with the outside (p. 348).

However, they noted that the effects on prisonization of these antecedents was not uniform. In particular, differential resistance and dissimilar problems seemed to moderate the effects of the antecedents on prisonization.

Several advancements in prisonization research were also made during the 1970s. Schwartz (1971) compared the effects of both pre-institutional and situational influences on prisonization in a sample of 194 delinquent boys. The situational factors included integration into prison primary groups, staff orientation, family contact, and length of confinement. Conformity to the inmate code was related to staff orientation and length of confinement. Pre-prison variables were numerous and involved race, residence, migration, age at commitment, family status, family relationships, number of siblings, number of brothers, age rank, IQ, achievement, school grades, school status, truancies, suspensions, number of arrests, number of arrests for violent offenses, age at first arrest, and prior commitments. However, only race, migration, age at commitment, number of arrests, number of arrests for violent offenses, and prior commitments were significantly associated with conformity to the inmate code. Thus, Schwartz (1971) demonstrated that pre-prison attributes were as strongly related to prisonization as situational deprivations.

Wellford's (1973) study of contact and commitment in a correctional community also discounted the indigenous influence of situational deprivations on prisonization. In particlar, he examined the relationship between an inmate's normative commitment to the inmate code and his position in a structure of interaction. Wellford discovered that the relationship between the degree of prisonization and an inmate's structural position (i.e., clique member or isolate) was non-significant. That is, the number of contacts that an inmate made inside prison did not influence his level of prisonization. This finding was contrary to the predictions of Clemmer (1940) and others who had maintained that primary group contacts were integral in the prisonization process.

The notion of self-consistency was another pre-prison characteristic of prisonization that several scholars investigated during the 1970s (Faine, 1973; Tittle, 1972). In particular, Faine (1973) developed a self-consistency approach to prisonization and tested it among a sample of 254 male inmates. Specifically, he examined antecedents of prisonization that were related to the self-concept, including reference group identification and social anchorage. Faine determined that those inmates who have self-concepts tied to legitimized social identities do not become prisonized. In fact, he found that individuals who enter prison with less stable self-conceptions become highly prisonized.

Jensen and Jones (1976) applied the findings from prior research on prisonization among male inmates to a female sample of convicts. They examined situational variables such as time spent in the institution, contact with outside friends and relatives, contact with staff, participation in special programs, and inmate interactions. Jensen and Jones also investigated the effects of non-institutional characteristics such as race, age, education, urban experience, previous incarceration, and legal status. Their findings supported Wheeler's (1961) interpretation of the temporal element of incarceration. Inmates in the middle phase of imprisonment were most likely to embrace attitudes contrary to staff expectations. However, age was most strongly and persistently related with nonconformist attitudes towards staff and the institution. Jensen and Jones (1973) concluded that "younger inmates, educated inmates, and inmates with urban backgrounds are more hostile towards the institution and its staff than older, less educated, nonurban inmates" (p. 594). Their research supports the contention that the antecedents of prisonization are the same for both male and female inmates.

A major advance in prisonization research involved Alpert's (1979) longitudinal analysis of 198 inmates. This was, in fact, a methodological accomplishment that had been suggested by prior researchers (e.g., see Atchley & McCabe, 1968; Wheeler, 1961). Alpert found that individual characteristics such as race, criminal record, and years in prison were significantly related to prisonization. For example, whites and nonwhites seemed to experience prisonization at different rates. Prisoners with more extensive records also exhibited higher degrees of prisonization. Lastly, Alpert determined that prisoners who had been incarcerated for over three years had different rates of prisonization than inmates who had been incarcerated for a shorter period of time. Thus, Alpert's general findings were consistent with Clemmer's (1940) contention that length of sentence is related to prisonization. Alpert's work can also be interpreted as moderately supportive of Wheeler's (1961) hypothesis that prisonization varies by phase of institutional career.

Lastly, a line of research initiated by Thomas (1971) summed up much inquiry on prisonization during the 1960s and 1970s. He outlined the two goals of his project as follows:

> First, there has been no adequate comparison of the deprivation and importation models. The primary goal of this research is to provide such a comparison. Second, it is reasonable to argue that these two models are not alternative perspectives on the same phenomena and that, instead, they should be viewed as complementary. Thus, a secondary purpose of this project is to present a more inclusive model of prisonization which is sufficiently general to subsume both the importation and the deprivation model (Thomas, 1971, p. 19).

The majority of the studies in the 1960s and 1970s seemed to be directed at debunking either the deprivation or importation model of subcultural formation. In fact, Thomas' (1971) entire dissertation project involved a test of these two analytical perspectives on adult resocialization in total institutions. He explored antecedents of prisonization that had been examined in prior research, including duration of exposure to the convict subculture, interpersonal involvement inside prison, alienation, social role adatpation, criminal identification, proportion of time served, pre-prison influences, and extra-prison expectations. In subsequent work, Thomas (1977) determined that years served, prior employment, post-prison expectations, and contextual powerless were associated with prisonization. Thomas, Petersen, and Zingraff (1978) confirmed that pre-prison characteristics and situational deprivations are both important antecedents of prisonization.

In sum, the indigenous influence and cultural drift theories have been advanced to explain prisonization into the inmate subculture. The determinants of socialization in correctional facilities have been well documented by extant scholarship. The micro antecedents of prisonization include time served (e.g., Clemmer, 1940; Haynes, 1948), proportion of time served (e.g., Atchley & McCabe, 1968; Wellford; 1967; Wheeler, 1961), primary group contacts (e.g., Clemmer, 1940; Haynes, 1948; Wheeler, 1961; Stratton, 1967), prior incarcerations (e.g., Morris & Morris, 1962; Tittle & Tittle, 1964; Wheeler, 1961), social role adaptations (e.g., Garabedian, 1963; Schrag, 1961; Sykes, 1958), the number of outside contacts (e.g., Morris & Morris, 1962), self-concept (Faine, 1973; Tittle, 1972), age (Jensen & Jones, 1976; Schwartz, 1971); and other pre-prison, sociodemographic characteristics (Schwartz, 1971). Most research on prisonization has focused on the individual predictors of socialization into the inmate subculture. The macro antecedents of prisonization are not nearly as well documented by prior scholarship.

### Macro Antecedents of Prisonization

The macro antecedents of prisonization include the contextual features of prisons that influence the rates of socialization into the inmate subculture. Extant research on the macro antecedents of prisonization has almost exclusively focused on the organizational structure of correctional institutions. Thomas and Petersen (1977) noted that these organizational settings are influenced by the following contextual features:

> The physical structure of the institution, the manner in which available resources are allocated, the rigid organizational hierarchy, lines of communication, the distribution of decision-making power, the routinization of organizational activities, the means by which organizational participants other than inmates are evaluated, and related characteristics and activities and characteristics of the organization (p. 37).

Likewise, many structural analyses of prison life have investigated two particular goals of correctional institutions, namely treatment and custody (see Adamek & Dager, 1968; Akers, Hayner, & Gruninger, 1977; Berk, 1966; Grusky, 1959; Mathiesen, 1971; Street, 1966; Street, Vinter, & Perrow, 1966; Wilson, 1968; Zald, 1962).

Prisonization implies an opposition to correctional staff and the institution. However, several scholars have attempted to specify the nature of the relationship between prisonization and the organizational goals (i.e., treatment versus custody) of correctional facilities. Grusky (1959) examined an experimental prison camp that stressed treatment goals. He found that inmate leaders in this treatment-oriented facility expressed prosocial attitudes toward the institution. Berk (1966) replicated Grusky's findings and extended this line of research. In particular, he investigated the relationship between the organizational goals of three minimum-security prisons and the convict subculture. He found that positive inmate attitudes toward the institution were related to the facility's support for treatment goals. Berk also made the following discovery:

> Inmates who had spent longer time in the custodially oriented prison were more likely to hold negative attitudes than those who had only been there a few months, whereas the reverse was true at the treatment-oriented prison where inmates who had spent a long time in the prison were more likely to hold positive attitudes than negative ones (p. 525).

He also determined that these contextual effects could not be accounted for by variation in the individual attributes of offenders. For instance, Berk noted that more serious offenders did not have more negative attitudes toward the facility than less serious offenders.

Street (1966) examined the inmate group in four correctional facilities for juvenile males. Two institutions focused on custodial goals, while two were treatment-oriented. He found that prisoners in the custodial facilities exhibited more negative attitudes toward the institution and appeared to be more prisonized. Conversely, Street (1966) discovered that "inmates in the treatment-oriented institutions more often expressed positive attitudes toward the institution and staff, non-prisonized views of adaptation to the institution, and positive images of self change" (p. 49). He also included individual variables (e.g., age, race, IQ, prior record, family status, urban-rural background, and social class) in the model to determine if the attitudinal differences were simply a reflection of individual variation. However, the institutional orientation still significantly affected prisonization when controlling for individual characteristics.

The effect of organizational goals on prisonization appears to apply cross-culturally as well. Akers, Hayner, and Gruninger (1977) conducted a cross-national study that was designed to examine the influence of institutional goals (i.e., treatment versus custody) on the aggregated rate of prisonization. They sampled 22 penitentiaries in the United States, Mexico, England, Germany, and Spain. Akers et al. distinguished between treatment-oriented and custodial facilities by rating the institutions on specific organizational dimensions. These dimensions included architecture, classification policy, use of inmate labor, ratios and quality of personnel, policy on freedom of outside contact for inmates, prison programs, etc. In general, Akers et al. (1977) determined that custodial institutions intensified feelings of degradation and punishment that were associated with higher rates of prisonization in all countries.

In sum, the macro antecedents of prisonization have typically been couched in the organizational structure of the correctional institutions. Treatment-centered facilities tend to foster more positive attitudes toward the institution, whereas custody-oriented compounds encourage negative inmate assessments of the prison. Additionally, Mathiesen (1971) suggested that maximum security facilities are more custodially-based, while minimum and medium security institutions are more treatment-oriented. This may explain why the pains of imprisonment were so pronounced in Sykes' (1958) study of the New Jersey State Maximum Security Prison. Consequently, the effects on inmate behavior of a prison's physical environment have seldom been explored in extant research (Sommer, 1971). However, Flynn (1976) suggested, but offered no empirical validation, that ecological factors such as lack of privacy, warehousing, crowding, and sensory deprivation may exacerbate deprivation and lead to boredom, restlessness, anxiety, hunger, cognitive inefficiencies (e.g., an inability to concentrate, think clearly, loss of contact with reality), speech impairments, emotionality, and temporal disorientations.

## Consequences of Prisonization

Socialization into the inmate subculture may have several detrimental consequences for inmates. In fact, prisonization has extra-institutional as well as intra-institutional effects. Clemmer (1950) suggested that "the culture of a prison influences the people participating in it, in the same way as culture anywhere plays a part in shaping the lives of men" (p. 313). Anticipating labeling theory, he proposed that imprisonment may actually be a source of criminality. The socialization process that inmates undergo inside prison may teach them more sophisticated and elaborate methods of breaking the law. In other words, incarceration may exacerbate criminal careers and breed crime. Clemmer was also one of the first scholars to relate prisonization with parole violations and recidivism.

Parole success is correlated with the quantity and quality of employment obtained by parolees more than any other factor (Dale, 1976; Knox, 1981). Homant (1984) suggested that prisonization decreases the likelihood that an ex-offender will secure employment upon release. He proposed that inmates initially lack self-esteem due to the degradation ceremonies associated with entry into a total institution. The inmate subculture provides an expedient way for inmates to regain their self-esteem and counteract the pains of imprisonment. Convicts come to depend upon the subculture and ignore alternate ways to build self-esteem. Once prisonization occurs, inmates are less likely to obtain job training or preparation that would help them secure employment upon release. However, when released, a prisonized inmate does not have the subculture from which to draw self-esteem and is ill-prepared to enter the workforce. Crime, leading to parole violations, may be the only means by which a highly prisonized inmate can survive on the outside.

Zingraff (1975) examined the relationship of prisonization to intra-institutional attitudes and post-prison expectations. He suggested that prisonization has three potential ramifications, including opposition to the formal organization of the institution, increased priority placed on in-group loyalty, and denial of the legitimacy of the legal system in general. He confirmed that prisonization was actually associated with oppositional attitudes towards the institution and the law, as well as negative post-release expectations. Prisonization was unrelated to increased in-group loyalty in his sample. Zingraff (1975) remarked that "the greater the degree of normative assimilation and the more negative the postrelease expectations of the inmate, the greater the probability that the effects of confinement will be negative" (p. 375). He concluded that prisonization is an inhibitor of effective resocialization in prison.

Prisonization also undermines therapeutic correctional programs. Peat and Winfree (1992) interviewed 72 drug abusers in a medium security correctional facility in order to determine if prisonization reduces participation in therapeutic services. They discovered that inmates in treatment reported lower levels of prisonization and the absence of a violent-crime conviction. Peat and Winfree (1992) concluded that:

> Prisonization and the traditional inmate subculture are antithetical to the goals of rehabilitation, including those proposed in most therapeutic communities ... Instead of participation in prison treatment and "self-improvement" programs, it mandates avoidance; instead of cooperation with prison officials, it mandates manipulation; instead of respect for middle-class values, it mandates derision (p. 209).

Socialization into the inmate subculture was associated with lower levels of treatment exposure. Thus, prisonization is not only an inhibitor of effective resocialization, it also impedes the delivery of therapeutic services to inmates.

Lastly, Cohen (1976) outlined several determinants of prison violence that are associated with the prisonization process. In particular, he suggested that the deprivations of imprisonment affect prison violence. Deprivations are also key determinants of prisonization. In fact, the inmate subculture is a response to the pains of imprisonment. Prisoners attempt to obtain material comforts such as food, alcohol, drugs, money, clothing, work assignments, and sex in order to counteract the deprivations of imprisonment. Most of these items are contraband in prison. As such, Cohen (1976) noted that the pursuit of illicit goods in prison may result in the following quandary:

If they [illicit goods] give rise to conflict and disputes as commerce (as we call it on the outside) and hustles (as we call it on the inside) invariably do, they cannot be settled by the invoking of services of legally constituted authority (p. 18).

An illicit inmate organization must then devise its own ways of securing justice, revenge, discipline, the collection of debts, and the enforcement of contracts. These informal means often involve violence or the threat of violence. Cohen (1976) suggested that "within the prison, likewise, the 'criminalization' of activities for which the demand nonetheless persists has the consequence of insuring the unauthorized use of force, that is, of violence" (p. 18). In this fashion, institutional misconduct and prison violence may result from the deprivations of imprisonment and the subcultural response to these collective problems.

## Criticisms of Prisonization

Although the concept of prisonization has been well documented by extant research, it is not without critics. Hawkins (1976) argued that research on prisonization has failed to yield any definitive findings. He implied that researchers studying prisonization have not demonstrated the utility or relevance of the concept. Hawkins (1976) remarked, in a rather essentialist tone, that prisonization has "suffered a death by a thousand qualifications, so attenuated that even now there are those unaware of its demise" (p. 63). In a related vein, Ramirez (1984) questioned whether the prisonization process actually represents a bonafide conflict between prison staff and inmates. He employed a social constructionist perspective and suggested that prisonization may be an artificial concept, not an empirical reality. Ramirez proposed that the notion of prisonization may be a construction on the part of early middle-class researchers who were attempting to explain lower-class adaptations to confinement. The oppositional assumption associated with the inmate code may simply be a function of their biases.

In a recent article, Leahy (1998) scrutinized the assumption of inmate solidarity that is at the heart of the prisonization hypothesis. She engaged in qualitative, in-depth interviews with 40 subjects from a maximum security institution. Leahy (1998) reached the following conclusions:

1. no solidarity among the inmates
2. no organized opposition to the administration
3. no organized violence
4. no meaningful rehabilitation taking place ...
5. modes of coping depended on the inmates construction of reality (their world view), and there was a concerted effort by all inmates to confine interaction with others inside the prison to a minimum
6. religion was an important factor in the coping strategies of some inmates
7. families played a central role in prisoners' constructions of reality and in their coping strategies (p. 289).

If valid, her study has dire consequences for prisonization research. However, there are reasons to believe that Leahy's results were biased and potentially fallacious. Given the small sample size, it is unlikely that her findings are generalizable to other prisoners. In fact, 22.5 percent of her initial sample declined to participate in the study, raising serious issues regarding sample selection bias. It simply could have been that those subjects who refused to participate were the most highly prisonized inmates. Also, no advanced statistical techniques were used to examine the concept of prisonization. Leahy's analysis consisted of snippets from her interviews. Although there are several methodological shortcomings in Leahy's research, it still potentially raises some concerns over the authenticity of prisonization as a subject of scientific investigation.

In sum, critics of prisonization have attacked two of its main normative assumptions. Ramirez (1984) discounted the oppositional assumption of the inmate code by claiming that inmates are not actually organized in opposition to correctional staff. Additionally, Leahy (1998) called the assumption of inmate solidarity into question when she alleged that prisoners are too self-interested to maintain group loyalties. However, the concept of prisonization may endure. It may be that inmates are socialized into smaller sub-groups in prison rather than one over-arching inmate subculture. Perhaps opposition is divided between custodial staff and rival groups, and perhaps solidarity in the contemporary prison is more specific and less general. In fact, current renditions of prison life imply that modern inmate sub-groups are different from the inmate subculture of the Big House. Yet, the micro mechanism that allows these new groupings to persist still involves enculturation into some type of social group.

## The Contemporary Prison

Salient problems in modern correctional facilities include prison crowding, drugs, and gangs. Pollock (1997) suggests that the growing prison population is related to hardline drug policies that were enacted in the United States during the last few decades. Likewise, Irwin and Austin (1994) maintain that America's new drug laws proscribe more punitive sentencing for drug offenders. Specifically, more drug offenders are being convicted and sentenced to prison. Consequently, the social makeup of the prison itself has changed. Inciardi, Lockwood, and Quinlan (1993) indicate that as many as 60 percent of inmates report using drugs in prison. Increased prison populations often result in over-crowded situations. Prison crowding is a structural condition of prisons that may affect individual relationships on the inside.

<u>Prison Crowding</u>
Research examining the effects of crowding on humans began in the early 1970s in response to animal studies that examined population density and social pathology. Calhoun (1962) created an experimental condition where the needs of its population surpassed its environmental resources. Specifically, Calhoun over-bred a colony of rats in a limited space. As a consequence of this overcrowding, he noted increases in socially disorganized behaviors such as aggression, mortality, and homosexuality. Crowding in prison may have similar detrimental effects or even exacerbate the effects of other deprivations (i.e., loss of liberty, loss of autonomy, etc.) on social processes such as prisonization and adaptation.
    Paulus, McCain, and Cox (1973) investigated crowing in custodial settings. They remarked that "prison environments provide an excellent setting in which to study the psychological effects of sustained exposure to a wide range of spatial and social density conditions" (Paulus et al.,

1973, p. 428). Prisons offer ideal field locations that allow researchers to examine the effects of crowding. First, prisons supply a wide variety of housing units and occupants. The different combinations of inmates in housing units allow for variation among measures of spatial and social density. Next, the nature of incarceration allows for ample long-term observations. Prison populations are also quite heterogeneous. Biographical data on subjects are accessible as well. Lastly, volunteer rates in prisons are typically good (Paulus et al, 1977).

Although findings are not entirely consistent, research tends to indicate that prison crowding is associated with several types of pathologies. Megargee (1977) used archival data from incident reports to link prison misconduct with population density. Specifically, density was significantly correlated with both the number and the rate of disciplinary reports filed. Farrington and Nuttall (1980) also examined prison crowding in relation to institutional misconduct and recidivism. They used archival data to illustrate a negative relationship between overcrowding and effectiveness. Farrington and Nutall (1980) hypothesized the following:

> It may be that prisoners are more likely to become contaminated by other prisoners in overcrowded conditions, or that it is more difficult to attempt rehabilitative activities in overcrowded conditions, or that the experience of living in an overcrowded prison produces stress and aggression (p. 230).

Their speculations are quite congruous with the deprivation model of subcultural formation.

Cox, Paulus, and McCain (1984) examined prison crowding using both archival and clinical data. They reached seven main conclusions. First, Cox et al. determined that increases in prison populations without increased housing were associated with more deaths, suicides, disciplinary infractions, and psychiatric commitments. In general, large institutions also yield higher rates of death, suicide, and psychiatric commitments. Third, double cells result in negative housing ratings, increased disciplinary infraction rates, and more complaints of illness. Negative psychological reactions and increased complaints of illness were both associated with large open dormitories. Fifth, multiple-occupant units were also related to low space per person, no privacy, the constant presence of others, and double-bunking. The negative effects of crowding can be reduced by placing privacy cubicles in open dormitories. Lastly, spatial density does not appear to produce long-term, detrimental effects.

Prison Gangs

The social organization inside prison has changed dramatically over the past few decades (Irwin, 1980; Pollock, 1997). The inmate contraculture of the contemporary prison substantially diverges from the convict subculture of the Big House. Rather than being characterized by one overarching inmate culture, the social organization inside prison today involves many smaller social units centered around issues such as race, criminal orientation, shared pre-prison experiences, shared prison interests, and forced proximity (Irwin, 1980). Irwin (1980) observed that "loyalty to other prisoners has shrunk to loyalty to one's clique or gang" (p. 194). Likewise, Hunt, Riegel, Morales, and Waldorf (1993) offered a similar statement concerning changes in prison culture. Most notably, they argued that the traditional inmate subculture has been replaced by new forms of social organization. In short, scholars now believe that the contemporary inmate subculture cannot be characterized as one consensus. Rather, it is comprised of many sociocultural sub-systems vying for power, goods, and services. These subcultures are now called gangs, and these gangs often have norms that may be different from the tenets of in-group loyalty and opposition to custodial authority that represented the traditional inmate code.

The prisonization process has adjusted in relation to the organizational changes that have occurred inside prison. Stevens (1997) develops a model of prisonization that takes the gang phenomenon into consideration. In fact, he argues that inmates, once incarcerated, still undergo a prisonization process. However, prisoners are now socialized into gangs rather than the convict subculture. Stevens (1997) notes that "subsequent incarceration promotes the social agents of gang participation through prisonization" (p. 25). Furthermore, he suggests that juvenile detention actually leads to further criminality and adult gang involvement.

Stevens (1997) proposes that "juveniles confined in closed institutions might share place-intensity experiences and gang affiliation agents through tip encounters when they are subjected to substandard environments and poor living conditions" (p. 25). Tips are groups of individuals from the same town or neighborhood who engage in similar types of delinquency (Irwin, 1980). In short, Stevens maintains that a process of socialization (i.e., juvenilization) begins at juvenile training facilities and results in adult prisonization into the gang world. To borrow an example from medicine, youth confined in juvenile detention centers become infected with a social pathogen (i.e., norms consistent with adult gangs) that develops into a full blown disease (i.e., violent gang alliances) if they become incarcerated as adults.

The social organization of the contemporary prison is quite different from that of the Big House. Most notably, the social units of inmate cohesion have changed. Some researchers have suggested that gang affiliations have replaced the traditional convict subculture (Irwin, 1980). However, inmates still undergo a process of prisonization whereby they learn the norms of the gang. In fact, the prisonization process may now begin in juvenile facilities, become fully activated in adult institutions, and culminate in gang allegiances.

**Sociologies of Imprisonment**

Early sociologists examined life inside the Big House. They viewed the emergence of the inmate subculture as a collective attempt to reduce the deprivations of prison life. The inmate code was the normative system of the inmate subculture, and its two key assumptions involved inmate solidarity and opposition to custodial authority. Prisonization was the process of assimilation into the inmate subculture whereby prisoners learned the tenets of the inmate code. However, Becker (1964) noted that "some inmates never take on criminal values" (p. 48). In fact, the extent to which prisoners take on the inmate code and behave accordingly depends upon a variety of individual traits and institutional features.

Both pre-prison characteristics and indigenous, institutional factors influence the extent to which convicts become involved with the inmate subculture. These antecedents of prisonization include a mixture of micro characteristics of prisoners and macro features of prisons. The micro antecedents of prisonization include time served, proportion of time served, primary group contacts, prior incarcerations, social role adaptations, the number of outside contacts, self-conception, age, and other pre-prison sociodemographic variables. The macro antecedents of prisonization involve the security level of the prison, its treatment orientation, and its physical layout. Furthermore, a high degree of prisonization is believed to be associated with intra-institutional problems, such as lower levels of treatment exposure, misconduct, and violence as well as extra-institutional difficulties such as general post-release adjustment problems, post-prison unemployment, parole violation, and recidivism.

Recent scholarship questions the authenticity of this interpretation of prison life today. In particular, Irwin (1980) argues that the Big House of the early twentieth century has been replaced by the contemporary prison. And Johnson (1996) notes "what was once a repressive but comparatively safe 'Big House' is now often an unstable and violent social jungle" (p. 133). Inmate allegiances have diminished, and gangs now dominate the social landscape. However, the process of prisonization is still believed to occur to some degree in correctional facilities. A primary goal of the current project is to assess the extent to which prisonization is still a bonafide social process inside correctional facilities. Also, this research should shed light on whether the antecedents that Clemmer (1940) specified still predict prisonization, or whether Irwin's (1980) notions about racial tension and gang activity are better explanations of prisonization in modern correctional institutions.

# CHAPTER 4

# The Multilevel Research Design

The current project involves a multilevel research design. In fact, the research questions dictated the use of this quantitative methodology. According to theory, subcultures emerge when individuals with similar problems interact with one another. Subcultures arise as collective solutions to individual problems. A key assumption of subcultural theory is that individuals within the same social groupings influence each other and orient their perspectives in anticipation of one another's actions. However, traditional single-level research designs are based on the assumption that individuals within the same social group are unrelated. In other words, traditional methodologies assume independence in the estimation of outcomes for individuals in the same groups or sociocultural sub-systems. Clearly, traditional research designs are not compatible with the central assumption of subcultural theory.

This chapter outlines the phases of a multilevel research project. First, the hierarchical nature of multilevel data and the steps taken to acquire this information are addressed. The sources of data and the sampling techniques used in this research are then discussed. Next, the analytic strategy behind the project and the full conceptual model are rendered. Lastly, the primary variables under investigation are specified, and the multilevel hypotheses are presented.

## Multilevel Data

Inmates are incarcerated within penitentiaries. As such, data gathered inside correctional facilities have an implicit hierarchical structure that includes lower-level observations from prisoners nested within the higher level of a prison. Information on prisoners comprise Level 1 data while Level 2 data consist of information on prisons. Convicts in one specific prison are exposed to the same contextual features of that particular institution. Specifically, they are all subjected to the same intake, routine, physical environment, and organizational structure. Due to their closeness in space, inmates share common experiences. Kreft and De Leeuw (1998) describe this phenomenon as an intra-class correlation. An intra-class correlation is a measure of similarity, or homogeneity, within groups and heterogeneity between groups.

Sources of Data

Both prisoners and prisons are units of analysis. Data for the current project came from two sources. A questionnaire for inmates was developed that tapped a variety of demographic, attitudinal, and behavioral information. Data on convicts were obtained by surveying 1,054 inmates in 30 prisons across Kentucky, Tennessee, and Ohio. Data collected on inmates in contemporary prisons contain variables that describe prisoners, such as race, attitudes towards staff, and prior criminality, as well as variables that tap prisoners' perception of context such as overcrowding. Information on prisoners comprise Level 1 data. However, responses from the prisoners' survey were also be aggregated to reveal unofficial Level 2 information . In addition to the aggregated data from Level 1, supplemental information on prisons was also needed. These data were solicited from the Departments of Corrections in each state. Thus, data for the current project came from both surveys of inmates and prison administration.

Level 1 Data Collection

The data collection process involved a number of preliminary steps. First, a survey instrument based on prior correctional research was needed. Upon completion, the final instrument was 10 pages in length and included two sections. Demographic and background data were secured in the first part while information on prison life (i.e., attitudes and behaviors) was acquired in the second. The next preliminary step of data collection involved obtaining approval from the Departments of Corrections in the sample states. Initially, correctional officials in Kentucky, Tennessee, Ohio, Indiana, and Virginia were contacted. Access to correctional facilities in Kentucky, Tennessee, and Ohio was granted, but admission to institutions in Indiana and Virginia was denied. Once permission from enough states had been secured, the project was presented to the Institutional Review Board (IRB) at the

University of Kentucky. After a full review and minor revisions to the instrument and consent form, IRB approval (i.e., 00-0637) was granted on November 11, 2000.

Field work began in January 2001 with a pilot study at Blackburn Correctional Complex in Lexington, Kentucky. Pilot studies are useful in survey methodology for troubleshooting purposes. It provided a chance to determine several important factors, including the length of time needed to administer and complete the survey, unclear or misleading questions, the reading aptitude of the subjects, etc. For instance, it was anticipated that the sub-samples would be partially illiterate. As such, it was decided that the surveys would be read aloud to subjects in small groups. However, inmates reacted negatively to this strategy. In particular, the subjects seemed withdrawn and insulted. One even remarked, "We're not stupid you know - we can read!" Subjects also voiced concerns about other inmates and correctional staff listening in and making incorrect assumptions as to their answers. The validity of the responses may have been compromised if survey administration had continued in this manner. As such, the subjects at Blackburn were allowed to break away from the small group and complete their surveys individually. Subsequent surveys were self-administered in the remaining 29 prisons.

Most subjects completed the self-administered survey in approximately 45 minutes. Some respondents needed as little as 30 minutes to fill out the survey while others took an hour and a half. Additionally, if an inmate had difficulty reading or writing, the researchers assisted him with the completion of his survey. Face-to-face interviews of this nature were rare, but usually took at least an hour and a half to complete. Altogether, it took approximately three months to collect data from 1,054 subjects imprisoned at 30 different correctional facilities across Kentucky, Tennessee, and Ohio.

## Level 2 Data Collection

In comparison to the work associated with the collection of data at Level 1, data collection at Level 2 was a relatively simple process. Measures describing the prison context from the inmates' point of view could be aggregated from Level 1 data. Additionally, supplemental Level 2 data were obtained from official sources. In particular, Carol Williams from the Commonwealth of Kentucky's Department of Correction, Jim

Wilson from the State of Tennessee's Department of Correction, and Lee Norton from the Ohio Department of Rehabilitation and Correction were instrumental in providing information on each of the correctional institutions under investigation in this study.

## Multilevel Sampling

Multistage cluster sampling is most likely the ideal sampling strategy for multilevel research. According to Bachman and Paternoster (1997), this technique involves "extracting a random sample of groups, collectivities, or clusters of elements that are available... [and then] ...sampling the individual elements of interest from within these selected cases" (p. 14). Multistage cluster sampling diminishes the introduction of bias into the sample by using successive random approximations. For example, a multistage cluster sample of U.S. prisoners would involve several steps. Initially, a first-order sample of states would have been randomly selected. Next, from within these states, a probability sample of prisons from those states would have been drawn. Finally, inmates who were incarcerated at each randomly selected prison within each randomly sampled state would have been randomly selected into sub-samples. The results of such a study would have minimal bias, and the results would be generalizable to all inmates incarcerated in U.S. prisons.

Unfortunately, the present sampling strategy was not based on multistage cluster sampling techniques. Rather, the sampling strategy was mixed. That is, it combined availability and systematic random sampling techniques. At the state and prison levels, availability sampling was used. A combination of availability sampling and systematic random sampling was employed at the inmate level. Availability samples are generally easier, more expedient, and more economical than multistage cluster samples. However, Bachman and Paternoster (1997) note that precision and accuracy are sacrificed with availability samples. They go on to say that availability or convenience samples are the least representative and generalizable type of samples. Furthermore, Bachman and Paternoster (1997) propose that "it is necessary to describe explicitly the sampling procedures used in the methodology section of research reports to acknowledge the nonrepresentativeness of the sample" (p. 17). Therefore, it must be openly acknowledge that the results of this research may be strongly biased, particularly by geographic location. However, it is possible to justify the use of such a sampling strategy.

The nested data structure implicit in multilevel research designs entails a large amount of data. It was not only necessary to get an adequate amount of respondents at Level 1, but it was also imperative to obtain an appropriate number of prisons at Level 2. In order to accomplish this task, the most straightforward method was to sample prisons in several contiguous states. Contiguous states were selected because they were more convenient. Additionally, this research is quite exploratory. That is, only one multilevel study of prison life has been conducted to date. It did not seem prudent to embark on a grand multistage strategy without some initial exploratory findings to merit such investigation. In sum, this mixed-availability sampling strategy may be justified by appealing to the project's data requirements and its exploratory nature.

In addition to these justifications, intentional bias was introduced into the sample. In particular, only inmates who had been continuously imprisoned for six months at the institution in which they were currently housed were allowed to participate in the project. This residency requirement was necessary to eliminate those inmates who were too new to the institutional milieu to be affected by contextual forces. Likewise, inmates in reception centers and medical institutions were excluded because prisoners are usually only kept at such facilities for short periods of time. The sample was also restricted to male correctional facilities because prior research has suggested that women experience imprisonment differently than men (MacKenzie, Robinson, & Campbell, 1989). A contextual comparison of men's versus women's adjustment to incarceration was beyond the scope of this project. Lastly, an availability sample was ultimately necessary in order to accommodate the different sampling procedures implemented in each state. The actual sampling procedures were not uniform across Kentucky, Tennessee, and Ohio.

## Sampling in Kentucky

Sampling in Kentucky involved a number of stages. First, the Department of Correction in Kentucky was petitioned for access into 11 of their prisons. Admission was granted into all 11 state men's prisons in Kentucky. Mrs. Carol Williams, the research coordinator at the Department of Correction in Kentucky, was integral to this project. She reviewed the protocol and initially approved it. Mrs. Williams also generated a list of inmates who had been incarcerated at each facility for at least one year. The numbers of inmates per institution varied from 33 to well over 2,000 subjects. These registers served as the sampling frame for Kentucky. Then, a systematic random sampling technique was used to select up to 250 inmates at each institution for inclusion into the final sample. If fewer than 250 inmates were on each register, then all inmates listed were solicited.

Once permission was granted and the final sampling frame was in hand, Mrs. Williams coordinated liaisons at each prison. Dates, times, and locations for survey administration were scheduled through these liaisons. During the second phase of the sampling procedure, letters were sent to the pre-selected inmates. Participation in this project was completely voluntary. In fact, no sort of incentive (i.e., money, candy bars, etc.) that could potentially have been coercive was allowed. The letters were sent en masse to the prison liaisons who, in turn, delivered the letters to the inmates via the mail delivery systems at each institution. The recruitment letters informed potential subjects of the nature of the research, the date, time, and location of survey administration, and the correctional staffer who was overseeing the project. Exactly 2,134 recruitment letters were delivered to inmates in Kentucky. However, only 388 inmates turned out to take the survey and become part of the Level 1 sample for this state.

### Sampling in Tennessee

Sampling in Tennessee was similar to the procedures followed in Kentucky with some minor changes. The Department of Correction in Tennessee granted permission to survey inmates in 9 prisons. However, one facility (i.e., Wayne County Boot Camp) was excluded because no inmates met the pre-qualification, residency criterion. Mr. Jim Wilson, the research coordinator at the Tennessee Department of Correction, was quite effectual in the implementation of this project in his state. He reviewed the proposal and obtained its approval from the Commissioner of the Department of Correction in Tennessee. Mr. Wilson also compiled a list of inmates who had been incarcerated at each facility for at least six months and established liaisons at each prison. The residency requirement was reduced to six months in order to boost the sampling frames. It was believed that, by reducing this stipulation, more inmates would be qualified to participate and thereby agree to take part in this project. The letters of solicitation for inmates in Tennessee were similar to the ones that we sent to subjects in Kentucky. The letters basically informed potential subjects of the goals, the date, time, and location of the study, and the correctional liaison who would be monitoring the administration of the survey. As many as 400 recruitment letters were sent out per institution for a total of 2,848 letters. However, only 300 inmates completed the survey in Tennessee.

## Sampling in Ohio

The sampling procedure in Ohio was unlike the techniques used in Kentucky and Tennessee. Access to 26 correctional facilities in Ohio was desired. However, Dr. Lee Norton, the research coordinator at the Ohio Department of Correction and Rehabilitation, recommended that the number of Ohio prisons in our Level 2 sample be reduced. As such, access to 11 of these correctional institutions was eventually obtained. Unlike Mrs. Williams or Mr. Wilson, Dr. Norton was unable to supply a list of inmates who had been incarcerated in his state's correctional system for at least six months. Therefore, systematic random sampling in Ohio's prisons was implausible.

Officials in Ohio also called for another pilot study at the Warren Correctional Complex after data collection had concluded in Kentucky. During this exercise, a convenience sampling strategy was tested. Dr. Norton assigned a prison liaison at each facility in Ohio. However, instead of delivering individual recruitment letters, these liaisons were responsible for posting a sign-up sheet in the dormitories at each facility. The posting described the study, explained the qualifications (i.e., at least six months of residency at that particular prison), and indicated the date, time, and location of the survey administration. In order to participate in the project, inmates were required to sign up in advance. It is impossible to estimate how many potential subjects were eligible to take part in this study. There is no way of knowing how many inmates had been incarcerated for at least six months at each prison or how many potential subjects actually noticed the sign-up sheet in their living quarters. In spite of this shortcoming, 366 inmates from Ohio completed the questionnaire.

Response Rates

Table 4.1 illustrates the response rates for the different prisons under investigation in the present study. The response rates in Kentucky ranged from a low of just above 7 percent at Luther Luckett Correctional Complex to a high of almost 85 percent at Bell County Forestry Camp. The mean response rate for correctional facilities in Kentucky was 18.18 percent. Tennessee's response rates extended from a low of 6.50 percent at the Turney Center Industrial Prison and Farm to a high of 16.50 percent at the Morgan County Correctional Complex. The average response rate for Tennessee prisons was 10.53 percent. However, it is impossible to know the true response rates in Ohio. Only raw numbers can be compared between the three states. As such, 388 inmates from 11 prisons in Kentucky, 300 subjects from 8 correctional facilities in Tennessee, and 366 prisoners from 11 institutions in Ohio were finally surveyed.

## Multilevel Modeling

Multilevel modeling, or hierarchical linear modeling (HLM), is perfectly suited for analyzing the social hierarchy of prisons. As previously mentioned, prisoners comprise Level 1 or the micro level of analysis. The macro Level 2 includes prisons. Multilevel models contain variables measured at both the micro and macro levels of this hierarchy. In fact, lower-level observations are nested within higher levels (Kreft & De-Leeuw, 1998). Each level of the hierarchy is represented by a separate statistical model. Bryk and Raudenbush (1992) elaborate as follows:

> With hierarchical linear models, each of the levels in this structure is formally represented by its own submodel. These submodels express relationships among variables within a given level, and specify how variables at one level influence relations occurring at another (p. 4).

In fact, Bryk and Raudenbush (1992) note that one of the primary applications of multilevel modeling involves the formulation and testing of hypotheses about cross-level effects, or how variables at one level affect relationships at another. Traditional analytic techniques are unable

Table 4.1

List of Prisons and Response Rates

| Prison | Number Responding | Letters Sent | Response Rate (%) |
|---|---|---|---|
| *Kentucky (n=11)* | | | |
| Bell County Forestry Camp | 28 | 33 | 84.85 |
| Blackburn Correctional Complex | 51 | 210 | 24.29 |
| Eastern Kentucky Correctional Complex | 54 | 250 | 21.60 |
| Frankfort Career Development Center | 22 | 102 | 21.57 |
| Green River Correctional Complex | 76 | 250 | 30.40 |
| Kentucky State Penitentiary | 20 | 250 | 8.00 |
| Kentucky State Reformatory | 34 | 250 | 13.60 |
| Luther Luckett Correctional Complex | 19 | 250 | 7.60 |
| Northpoint Training Center | 36 | 250 | 14.40 |
| Roeder Correctional Complex | 27 | 64 | 42.19 |
| Western Kentucky Correctional Complex | 21 | 225 | 9.33 |
| | | | |
| *Tennessee (n=8)* | | | |
| Middle Tennessee Correctional Complex | 21 | 280 | 7.50 |
| Morgan County Correctional Complex | 66 | 400 | 16.50 |
| Riverbend Maximum Security Institution | 20 | 168 | 11.90 |
| Northeast Correctional Complex | 33 | 400 | 8.25 |
| Northwest Correctional Complex | 62 | 400 | 15.50 |
| South Central Correctional Complex | 37 | 400 | 9.25 |
| Southeastern Tennessee State Regional Correctional Facility | 35 | 400 | 8.75 |
| Turney Center Industrial Prison and Farm | 26 | 400 | 6.50 |
| | | | |
| *Ohio (n=11)* | | | |
| Chillicothe Correctional Institution | 46 | n/a | n/a |
| Dayton Correctional Institution | 10 | n/a | n/a |
| London Correctional Institution | 46 | n/a | n/a |
| Madison Correctional Institution | 12 | n/a | n/a |
| Noble Correctional Institution | 53 | n/a | n/a |
| Orient Correctional Institution | 26 | n/a | n/a |
| Pickaway Correctional Institution | 16 | n/a | n/a |
| Ross Correctional Institution | 50 | n/a | n/a |
| Southeastern Correctional Institution | 29 | n/a | n/a |
| Southern Correctional Institution | 41 | n/a | n/a |
| Warren Correctional Institution | 37 | n/a | n/a |

to specify these cross-level effects in a statistically appropriate fashion.

Furthermore, hierarchical linear modeling is preferable to traditional regression analyses when examining micro phenomena that are naturally nested within macro contexts. Ordinary least squares (OLS) regression assumes independent terms. That is, traditional analytic techniques assume that observations are independent of one another. Ordinary least squares cannot account for intra-class correlations in natural hierarchies. Kreft and DeLeeuw (1998) describe an intra-class correlation as "the degree to which individuals share common experiences due to closeness in space and/or time" (p. 9). An intra-class correlation is a measure of similarity, or homogeneity, within groups and heterogeneity between groups. This intra-context dependency violates the assumption of independence in conventional regression analyses. Using traditional regression equations with units containing intra-class correlations inflates the alpha level and increases the probability for a type I error. Hierarchical linear models provide a more conservative test of significance.

Hierarchical linear modeling corrects for the intraclass correlation by employing submodels to account for variables at both levels of analysis. The models are fitted. First-level models are joined by a second-level model. Kreft and DeLeeuw (1998) note that the regression coefficients of the Level 1 model are then regressed on the Level 2 independent variables. Morevoer, Wilcox Rountree and Land (1996) summarize an important point:

> Hierarchical linear or logistic regression models account for the implicit hierarchy of data by employing submodels - each of the levels in the structure of the hierarchy is represented with its own submodel. These submodels, along with nested error terms, can account for effects and sources of variation at each of the levels of analysis represented in that data (p. 1357)

Hierarchical linear modeling estimates the coefficients more precisely because the models at multiple levels are linked together. In fact, when the Level 1 equation is combined with the Level 2 model, error terms from both levels are included into the combined HLM regression formula. The error variances are partitioned between the micro and the macro level. Traditional analytic models can only account for variance at one level.

Multilevel modeling is the most appropriate method for representing the social hierarchy of prison and exploring cross-level effects.

Although hierarchal linear modeling is most likely the best technique for analyzing nested data, Kreft and De Leeuw (1998) also review the traditional contextual model, the Cronbach model, and the ANCOVA model. Traditional contextual models employ either total/pooled regression or aggregate regression. Total regression is a precursor to multilevel modeling that involves estimating individual observations over the total group. Aggregate regression refers to performing a regression over the Level 2 means. This type of analysis disregards all within-prison variations, and thus the results cannot be used to explain Level 1 outcomes. Prediction is limited to the secondary level only. The Cronbach model involves centering individual-level variables around their group means which, in turn, forms a variable that is orthogonal to the centered group-level variables. Unfortunately, this technique still does not correct for the underestimation of standard error and the potential for a type 1 error. Lastly, the analysis of covariance (ANCOVA) model is the most statistically sound of the three alternatives discussed. It includes micro and macro data into one model, but specifies dummy codes for the macro variables. ANCOVA can show if individual-level characteristics vary over macro contexts; however, it cannot explain which macro qualities explain the variation. HLM remains a superior technique for analyzing nested data structures in detail.

Conceptual Model

The conceptual model consists of variables measured at two levels of analysis: prisoners and prisons. In particular, the micro and macro antecedents of prisonization and a micro consequence of the phenomenon are of particular interest. The explanatory variables at both Level 1 and Level 2 are derived from the deprivation and importation theories of subcultural formation that were reviewed in Chapter 3. Deprivation variables should operate at both levels of analysis. The dependent variables are prisonization and institutional misconduct. Control and explanatory variables at Level 1 pertain to characteristics of prisoners and include age, race, prior incarcerations, prior violent offenses, prior gang involvement, situational problems, sentence length, time served, degree of outside contacts (i.e., visits and letters from family and friends), prison of outside contacts (i.e., visits and letters from family and friends), prison friendships, deviant prison associates, perception of crowding, self-esteem, general definitions toward the rules, coping difficulties, and religious involvement inside prison. From cultural drift theory, age, race, prior incarcerations, prior violent offenses, and prior gang involvement are the primary importation variables. The main deprivation variables at the micro level from indigenous influence theory include situational problems, sentence length, time served, amount of outside contacts, prison friendships, deviant prison associates, and perception of crowding. Self-esteem, general definitions toward the rules, coping difficulties, and involvement in religious programs are included as controls.

Control and explanatory variables at Level 2 involve features of prisons such as the age of the institution, its security level, the numbers of education and vocation programs, crowding, gang presence, percentage non-white, percentage under 25 years old, population, staff-to-inmate ratio, and location (i.e., Kentucky, Tennessee, Ohio). Variables from official sources include the age of the institution, its security level, the number of education and vocational programs, crowding, the percentage non-white, the percentage under 25 years old, total population, and inmate-to-staff ratio. Gang presence was aggregated from survey responses. Also, dummy variables for each state were included in the model to test for differences in the mean levels of prisonization and institutional misconduct across the states.

Mathematical Equations

Both dependent variables in the current project are continuous in nature. As such, it is feasible to speculate that the micro and macro antecedents have a linear relationship to the outcome variables. This association may be represented in terms of two mathematical equations, one for each level of the analysis. The general equations for the Level 1 and Level 2 models are written as follows:

$$Y_{ij} = \beta_{0j} + \beta_{1j}X_{1ij} + ... \beta_{kj}X_{kij} + e_{ij} \qquad \textit{Level 1 Equation} \qquad (4.1)$$
$$\beta_{kj} = \Theta_{k0} + \Theta_{k1}W_{1j} + ... \Theta_{kq}W_{qj} + U_{kj} \qquad \textit{Level 2 Equation} \qquad (4.2)$$

Equation 1 is the within prison model and uses micro data collected from the survey of inmates, whereas equation 2 is the between prison model and calls for aggregate or prison-level data. The antecedent model of prisonization can be specified from this general equation 4.1. The consequential model of institutional misconduct includes the antecedents of prisonization plus prisonization itself. The antecedent model of prisonization is characterized by the following equation:

$$(\text{Prisonization})_{ij} = \beta_{0j} + \beta_{1j}(\text{age})_{ij} + \beta_{2j}(\text{race})_{ij} + \beta_{3j}(\text{prior incarcerations})_{ij}$$
$$+ \beta_{4j}(\text{prior violent offenses})_{ij} + \beta_{5j}(\text{prior gang involvement})_{ij} +$$
$$\beta_{6j}(\text{situational problems})_{ij} + \beta_{7j}(\text{sentence length})_{ij} + \beta_{8j}(\text{time served})_{ij} +$$
$$\beta_{9j}(\text{visits})_{ij} + \beta_{10j}(\text{letters})_{ij} + \beta_{11j}(\text{prison friendships})_{ij} + \beta_{12j}(\text{deviant prison}$$
$$\text{associates})_{ij} + \beta_{13j}(\text{perception of crowding})_{ij} + \beta_{14j}(\text{self-esteem})_{ij} +$$
$$\beta_{15j}(\text{general definitions toward the rules})_{ij} + \beta_{16j}(\text{coping difficulties})_{ij} +$$
$$\beta_{17j}(\text{religious involvement})_{ij} + e_{ij} \tag{4.3}$$

where $\beta_{0j}$ is the intercept or the mean level of prisonization for prison "j". The regression coefficients (i.e., $\beta_{1j}$, $\beta_{2j}$, $\beta_{3j,}$ etc.) represent the effects of micro-level variables on prisonization. The regression coefficients indicate the effect of one explanatory variable on prisonization while controlling for the others. The information in brackets signifies the micro-level predictors of prisonization. Lastly, $e_{ij}$ is the micro-level error term.

When proceeding to the second level model, the first step is to determine if any micro-level parameters vary across macro-level units. In other words, it is necessary to determine if the mean level of prisonization or the effects of the antecedents vary across prisons. If micro-level parameters do not vary in their effects across Level 2, then they are fixed. These fixed, micro-level parameters are specified as follows:

$$\beta_{kj} = \Theta_{k0} \tag{4.4}$$

However, each micro-level parameter may vary across prisons (i.e., macro-level units). In this case, the individual-level parameters that vary across contexts are specified as random in the following general manner:

$$\beta_{kj} = \Theta_{k0} + U_{kj} \tag{4.5}$$

If the effects of each antecedent varies across macro-level units, then a full random coefficients regression model can be used to represent this variation. However, it is more likely that only particular micro-level effects will vary across prisons. As such, a reduced random coefficients model with both fixed non-significant slope coefficients and significant random coefficients is more appropriate.

The next stage of hierarchical linear modeling involves specifying a Level 2 contextual model that uses prison-level variables to explain the variation in the effects of the individual-level antecedents on prisonization across contexts. In this contextual model, the individual-level specification is similar to equation 4.3. However, the prison-level equations may take on several forms, depending on which variables are significantly related to the micro-level relationship. For example, if the effect of situational problems (i.e., $\beta_{6j}$) on prisonization varies across different correctional institutions, then the following full Level 2 model for situational problems would be tested:

$\beta_{6j} = \Theta_{60} + \Theta_{61}$(age of prison)$_j + \Theta_{62}$(security level)$_j + \Theta_{63}$(number of vocational and educational programs)$_j + \Theta_{64}$(crowding)$_j + \Theta_{65}$(gang presence)$_j + \Theta_{66}$(percent non-white)$_j + \Theta_{67}$(percent under 25 years old)$_j + \Theta_{68}$(population)$_j + \Theta_{69}$(staff-to-inmate ratio)$_j + \Theta_{610}$(Kentucky) $+ \Theta_{611}$(Tennessee) $+ U_{6j}$  (4.6)

$\beta_{kj} = \Theta_{k0}$ for k=0-5, 7-17  (4.7)

Due to sample size restrictions, it may be impossible to estimate equation 4.6 as written. The Level 2 variables may have to be examined in a step-wise fashion with non-significant effects dropped. Yet, this example (i.e., equation 4.6) shows significant non-random variation of the effects of situational problems on prisonization. $\beta_{6j}$ is the product of the grand slope (i.e., $\Theta_{60}$) and the interaction of the prison-level variables (i.e., $\Theta_{61}$ through $\Theta_{611}$) with situational problems plus Level 2 error (i.e., $u_{6j}$). In this equation, $\Theta_{60}$ is the grand slope of situational problems or its average effect on prisonization; $\Theta_{61}$ through $\Theta_{611}$ represent the influence of macro variables on the effect of situational problems on prisonization when controlling for other variables. In this example, all other parameters (i.e., $\beta_{kj}$'s for k=0-5, 7-17) non-significantly varied across prisons and were thus specified as fixed.

**Statistical Software**

Many software programs are available to analyze multilevel data with hierarchical linear models. These statistical packages include HLM, VARCL, BMDP5-V, MLn, PROC MIXED, MIXOR and MIXREG (Kreft & DeLeuuw, 1998). MLn for the Windows operating system, also known as MlwiN, was chosen for this project. Kreft and DeLeuuw (1998) note that the MLn programs were developed by the Multilevel Project at the University of London. In addition, up to 15 levels of data with crossed and nested structures can be analyzed with MLn.

However, the program does come with a few minor caveats. First, the program simply will not run with missing data. As such, the group mean was substituted for missing ordinal and interval/ratio variables and scales. The group mode was substituted for missing data for nominal level variables. Secondly, all independent variables at Level 1 and Level 2 were centered by their grand means. Bryk and Raudenbush (1992) suggest that centering improves estimation and makes regression coefficient more readily interpretable. In sum, MLN is the statistical software used to analyze complete, centered multilevel data in the present study.

**Measures of Variables**

This multilevel investigation of social relations inside prison contains a number of variables. In particular, two outcomes of life inside prison are explored: prisonization and institutional misconduct. Micro and macro antecedents of prisonization are also tested. At Level 1, five variables come from the importation model of subcultural formation and eight are related to deprivation theory. Institutional misconduct is the primary outcome of prisonization, and it is predicted by eighteen individual-level and twelve prison-level variables. In the following section, the measurements and the metrics of all variables in the model are rendered. Table 4.2 displays the descriptive statistics for all variables in the conceptual model.

Dependent Variables
The two main dependent variables for the current project are prisonization and institutional misconduct. In fact, the first part of this study involves

Table 4.2

Descriptive Statistics for All Variables in the Conceptual Model

| Variables | Mean | S.D. | Low | High |
|---|---|---|---|---|
| *Dependent Variables* | | | | |
| Prisonization Index | 40.51 | 10.51 | 11.00 | 66.00 |
| Institutional Misconduct | 1.58 | 3.48 | .00 | 50.00 |
| | | | | |
| *Level 1 Independent Variables* | | | | |
| Age | 35.89 | 10.02 | 18.00 | 71.00 |
| Race | .44 | .50 | .00 | 1.00 |
| Prior Incarcerations | 2.11 | 3.84 | .00 | 40.00 |
| Prior Violence | .26 | .44 | .00 | 1.00 |
| Prior Gang Involvement | .12 | .32 | .00 | 1.00 |
| Situational Problems Index | 37.83 | 9.58 | 15.00 | 60.00 |
| Sentence Length | 22.94 | 23.91 | .50 | 263.00 |
| Time Served | 7.33 | 5.94 | .16 | 54.00 |
| Visits from Family/friends | 2.73 | 1.56 | 1.00 | 5.00 |
| Letters from Family/friends | 4.35 | 1.11 | 1.00 | 5.00 |
| Prison Friendships | 1.52 | .99 | .00 | 3.00 |
| Deviant Prison Friends | 1.09 | 1.76 | .00 | 6.00 |
| Perception of Crowding | 1.96 | 1.02 | .00 | 3.00 |
| Self-esteem Index | 47.08 | 9.55 | 10.00 | 60.00 |
| Definitions Index | 12.73 | 3.57 | 4.00 | 20.00 |
| Coping Difficulties Index | 16.79 | 6.22 | 8.00 | 32.00 |
| Religious Involvement | .48 | .50 | .00 | 1.00 |
| | | | | |
| *Level 2 Independent Variables* | | | | |
| Age of Prison | 25.93 | 23.28 | 5.00 | 117.00 |
| Security Level | .13 | .35 | 0.00 | 1.00 |
| Programs | 8.10 | 4.16 | 2.00 | 18.00 |
| Crowding | 1.00 | .11 | .83 | 1.39 |
| Gang Presence | .05 | .05 | .00 | .17 |
| Percent Nonwhite | .43 | .13 | .08 | .67 |
| Percent Under Age 25 | .18 | .10 | .06 | .51 |
| Population | 1274.00 | 607.00 | 190.00 | 2281.00 |
| Inmate-to-staff Ratio | 5.11 | 1.43 | 2.08 | 8.72 |
| Kentucky | .37 | .49 | .00 | 1.00 |
| Tennessee | .26 | .45 | .00 | 1.00 |
| Ohio | .37 | .49 | .00 | 1.00 |

examining the antecedents of prisonization (i.e., imported qualities and prison deprivations). Then, prisonization will itself become an independent variable predicting general misconduct. It is hypothesized that prisonization will significantly predict misconduct inside prison.

Prisonization was conceptualized as endorsement of the inmate code. Thomas' (1971) inmate code scale was modified to tap this facet of prisonization. His original version consisted of a summed scale of fourteen Likert-type attitudinal measures with a mean of 40.03 and a standard deviation of 10.55. The inmate code scale used in the current project is a summed index of eleven Likert-type measures with a mean of 40.51 and a standard deviation of 10.51. The response categories were strongly agree, moderately agree, slightly agree, slightly disagree, moderately disagree, and strongly disagree. Factor analysis was performed on the original fourteen items using data from a pilot study. Three of Thomas' original items were deleted due to unstable factor loadings. The remaining eleven items were summed to form the prisonization index used in this report. Originally, the lower the score obtained in this index, the higher the degree of inmate code adoption and prisonization. However, the response categories were recoded so that higher scores on this measure now indicate greater prisonization. Additionally, the alpha of .77 on this scale suggests that it is a moderately reliable measure. Furthermore, its frequency distribution and skewness statistic (i.e., -.144) suggest a normal distribution for this variable.

In the current project, institutional misconduct is treated as a primary consequence of prisonization. The reaction to misconduct by correctional staff is an integral element of the prisonization process. As such, institutional misconduct was measured by a single, continuous item that asked subjects, "how many 'tickets' or rule violations have you received in the past 12 months while in prison?" The average number of tickets received by subjects was 1.58 with a standard deviation of 3.48 and a range of 0 to 50 violations. The variable appears to be significantly skewed. Its skewness statistic was rather high (i.e., 6.174). As such, the variable's natural logarithm was used in the multivariate analysis. The mean for logged rule violations was .59 for the entire sample. The skewness statistic was reduced from 6.174 to .411 after the logarithmic transformation.

Level 1 Independent Variables

The explanatory variables at the micro-level of analysis consist of individual measures of importation and deprivation. As previously mentioned, importation variables include age, race, prior incarcerations, prior violence, and prior gang involvement. Situational problems, sentence length, time served, letters and visits from family and friends, prison friendships, deviant inmate associates, and the perception of crowding are all deprivation measures. Also, several control variables (i.e., self-esteem, definitions, coping difficulties, and religious involvement) were included in the conceptual model.

The age of each subject was assessed by a single item on the survey that asked, "what is your age?" This continuous measure was simply their chronological age in years. The average age of prisoners in our total sample (n=1054) was 35.89. The youngest inmate we surveyed was 18 and our oldest subject was 71 years old. This measure could have possible been influenced by our residency requirement of 6 months to a year, but it is unlikely since most inmates have sentences of at least one year.

Initially race was tapped by a closed-ended question with five categories that asked, "how would you best describe yourself?" The response categories included white, African-American or Black, Hispanic or Latino, Asian, or other. The majority of our subjects were white (i.e., 56 percent). African-Americans represented 39 percent of the total sample. The remaining five percent included Hispanics, Asians, and subjects who reported some other racial or ethnic background. This measure was subsequently recoded into a dichotomous variable with two categories: white and nonwhite.

Approximately 61 percent of the sample had previously been incarcerated as an adult. According to Table 4.2, the average number of prior adult incarcerations  was 2.11 with a low of 0 and a high of 50 priors. The question used to measure this variable simply asked respondents, "not counting this current incarceration, about how many prior times have you been incarcerated as an adult?" Additionally, about 26 percent of survey respondents indicated that they were previously incarcerated for a violent offense. This measure of prior violence was tapped by asking subjects, "prior to this incarceration, have you ever served time for a violence offense (for example: homicide, rape, robbery, assault, etc.)?" According to importation theory, prisoners with more extensive criminal backgrounds should be more highly prisonized and engage in more acts of institutional misconduct.

The final importation variable explored at the micro level involves prior gang activity. Subjects were asked to indicate the extent to which they participated in gang activities during the year prior to their current incarceration. The response categories included never, seldom, often, and always. These response categories were recoded as simply no and yes. A great majority of the sample (i.e., 88 percent) indicated that they never participated in gang activities on the street. In fact, about 12 percent admitted to gang involvement on the street, and only about 5 percent of the sample reported some type of gang involvement inside prison within the past year of incarceration.

Several variables, derived from deprivation theory, have been included in the current project. In particular, one of the main independent constructs involves a fifteen item index that taps the perceived situational problems and needs of offenders. This instrument was developed by Richards (1978) to assess the needs of long-term male prisoners. MacKenzie, Robinson, and Campbell (1989) refined the measure and tested it among a sample of female inmates. Specifically, the inmates were asked to indicate how difficult it has been for them to handle a series of problems during the last 12 months while incarcerated. Response categories included the following: very easy to handle, easy to handle, difficult to handle, and very difficult to handle. Fifteen items were combined into one additive scale measuring the perceived situational problems of prison life. The alpha of .88 indicates that this index is highly reliable. In fact, no higher alpha could have been attained by deleting any of the items. Furthermore, as indicated by Table 4.2, this scale ranges from 15 to 60 with a mean of 37.83. Higher scores on this index suggest more situational problems perceived inside prison.

Sentence length and time served are also derived from deprivation theory. Sentence lengths ranged from as little as 6 months for some inmates to as much as 263 years for others. The average sentence length for the sample was almost 23 years. Some inmates had served 54 years of this sentence while others had served only a few months. On average, subjects had served over 7 years of their current sentence. Wheeler (1961) suggested that inmates who are at different phases of their institutional careers report different levels of prisonization. As such, sentence length and time served should be important predictors of prisonization. A quadratic term for time served was also included in the multivariate analysis to determine if the effect of time served on the dependent variables was non-linear.

Prisonization research also focuses on the various social relationships in which inmates engage. Scholars have examined the stripping of outside contacts and the establishment of friendships and associations inside prison. A measure developed by Aday and Webster (1979) was used to tap outside contacts. Subjects were asked two questions: in the past 12 months in prison, how often have you received visits from family members or friends and in the past 12 months, how often have you received letters from family members or friends? The response categories included never, one or two times in the past year, three to six times in the past year, seven to twelve times in the past year, or over twelve times in the past year. Most inmates (i.e., 68.7 percent) reported some degree of visitation by their families and friends. However, 31.3 percent indicated that they received no visitations during the past twelve months in prison. In contrast, only 3.5 percent of the sample received no letters from family or friends during the past year. In fact, 68.7 percent reported receiving over twelve letters from families and friends in the last twelve months. Both measures were included as indicators of outside contacts.

The extensiveness of close friendships formed inside prison was measured by a question developed by Wheeler (1961). Inmates were asked, "have you developed any close friendships with other inmates since you have been incarcerated?" The responses were no, yes (1 or 2), yes (3 to 5), and yes (more than 5). The mean degree of prison friendships was 1.52, and the modal number was 1. This indicates that, on average, most inmates reported that they formed at least one close friendship inside prison. Only 15.5 percent of the sample reported forming no close friendships with other inmates while inside prison. Furthermore, subjects were asked, "in the last 12 months, how many of your six closest friends in prison have done something for which they were formally charged or could have been charged?" This question taps the extent to which a subject associates with troublemakers and more deviant inmates. On average, subjects reported that at least one of their close friends in prison was charged or could have been charged for a rule violation.

Crowding may be a powerful force inside prison. In fact, official measures of crowding may be easily manipulated by prison officials. The capacities set by internal committees or even the American Correctional Association are arbitrary, and the numbers of prisoners usually hover just around these guidelines. In order to get a perspective on crowding from the actual inhabitants of the prisons, inmates were asked, "do you believe that the institution where you are currently serving time is not crowded at all, slightly crowded, moderately crowded, or extremely crowded?" Many inmates (39.6 percent) reported extremely crowded living conditions inside prison. Moreover, only 10.8 percent of the sample indicated that their institution was not crowded at all. By and large, the vast majority of subjects (89.2 percent) maintained that their prison was crowded.

A measure of self-esteem was included in the model as a control variable since prior research has noted a link between self-esteem and prisonization (Tittle, 1972). Rosenberg's (1986) New York State Self-Esteem Scale was modified. All 10 items were used, but the response categories were expanded to reflect strongly agree, moderately agree, slightly agree, slightly disagree, moderately disagree, and strongly disagree. Given the high reliability (alpha = .82), all ten items were summed to form a single index. In fact, Rosenberg (1986) reports that previous studies of self-esteem in contexts other than prison have yielded reliability coefficients as high as .88 on this scale. Additionally, responses were recoded so that higher scores on this measure actually indicate lower levels of self-esteem. The scores ranged from a low of 10 to a high of 60 with a mean of 47.08.

Another control variable was included in this study to account for the subjects' general definitions about prison rules. A 4-item measure of individual definitions toward the law from Burton, Cullen, Evans, and Dunaway's (1994) test of differential association was adapted. In particular, the wording was changed somewhat in order to assess the inmate's more general definitions about the rules. Inmates where asked how characteristic of themselves were four statements. The response categories included the following choices: very much like me, unlike me, does not apply to me, like me, and very much like me. The reliability coefficient for this scale was rather low at .60, whereas Burton et al. (1994) reported an alpha of .71 for their original scale. In the present study, this index ranged from 4 to 20 and had a mean of 12.73. Higher scores on this measure indicate more prosocial definitions towards the rules.

MacKenzie et al. (1989) suggested that some inmates may be unable to cope with the problems inside prison. In fact, some prisoners may internalize the situational problems of prison life and become withdrawn and even suicidal. Thus, it is important to control for the differences in coping abilities among inmates. MacKenzie et al. specified a coping difficulties scale that included 8 items. The response categories were identical to the Situational Problems Scale. All 8 items were summed into one scale with a reliability coefficient of .87, a range of 8 to 32, and a mean of 16.79.

Leahy (1998) noted that religion was also an important coping strategy for inmates during imprisonment. A single item measure was included to control for the effect of religious involvement on prisonization. Subjects were asked whether they had been involved in religious services during the last 12 months in prison. Responses were simply recorded as either yes or no. The sample was almost divided on this measure with 48 percent indicating some involvement in religious services during the last year in prison.

Level 2 Independent Variables

Unlike the individual-level independent variables, the explanatory variables at the prison-level of analysis only consist of deprivation and control measures. Deprivation measures include the age of the prison, its security level, the number of educational and vocational programs, crowding, the presence of gangs, the percent nonwhite, and the percent under age 25. Three control variables (i.e., population, inmate-to-staff ratio, and location) were also included in the analysis. Most of these variables were obtained from the Departments of Correction in Kentucky, Tennessee, and Ohio. The gang presence variable was aggregated from survey data.

The age of each prison was calculated by subtracting the year in which it was built from the current year (i.e., 2001). The age of the institution is believed to be an indicator of deprivation because the living conditions in older facilities are likely to be less comfortable than newer prisons. Likewise, the concept of deterrence was built into the architecture of older prisons. The Kentucky State Reformatory (KSR) is a prime example of the poor living conditions and ominous architecture indicative of older prison systems. In fact, Anderson (2000) recounts one inmates' description of the living conditions at KSR in 1978 as follows:

> [The] place was nasty . . . There were roaches and rats. The building leaked when it rained, and you nearly froze to death in cold weather. We were stacked like cordwood, with no room to move. Half the toilets didn't work, and there weren't enough of them to begin with. I wasn't raised under these conditions, and it made me mad when I realized what the state was subjecting me too. People treat their livestock better than we were treated. The whole place was really a mess. The way I felt, for them to have killed me would have been an act of mercy (p. 2).

Undoubtably prison conditions at the Kentucky State Reformatory have improved in the past 23 years. However, the fact remains that some prisons included in this sample are only 5 years old, and do not have the reputations or legacies associated with places such as KSR. Indeed, the correctional facilities examined in the present study ranged from 5 to 117 years old. The average age of prisons in this sample was almost 30 years. KSR was built in 1937 and is 64 years old. The oldest correctional facility that we canvassed was the Kentucky State Penitentiary which was constructed in 1884. Noble Correctional Institution in Ohio was built in 1996 and was the youngest prison in our sample.

Research suggests that rates of prisonization are higher in custodial or maximum security institutions (Berk, 1966; Grusky, 1959; Mathiesen, 1971; Street, 1966). A dummy variable was used to distinguish non-maximum security institutions (i.e., coded as 0) from maximum security institutions (i.e., coded as 1). Four prisons, comprising about 13.3 percent of the sample, are classified as maximum security institutions. These facilities generally house inmates who have committed serious, violent offenses. Typically, the death house is also located at a maximum security institution in states that have capital punishment. For example, the Kentucky State Penitentiary, which happens to be the oldest prison in the sample, is also the site where prisoners who have been convicted of a capital crime are put to death. All three states in our sample currently endorse capital punishment.

Prisons that offer educational and vocational programs may be more therapeutic than facilities with fewer programmatic services. The number of educational and vocational programs was simply a continuous measure of all such programs at each institution. On average, prisons had 8.10 programs available for inmates. Bell County Forestry Camp in Kentucky had the fewest programs with only 2, while Northwest Correctional Complex in Tennessee had the most with 18 vocational and educational programs.

Crowding was measured at the levels of both the prison and the individual. At the macro-level, crowding was calculated by dividing the average daily population of each prison by its operational capacity. As indicated by Table 4.2, the mean crowding ratio is 1.00 which indicates that prisons in this sample were, on average, not crowded by official definitions. However, crowding ranged from a low of .83 at London Correctional Institution in Ohio to a high of 1.39 at Ross Correctional Institution in Ohio.

The presence of gangs at each institution could not be assessed through official sources. As such, it was necessary to aggregate survey data to get an approximation of gang activity inside each prison. In the survey, inmates were asked how often they had been engaged in gang activities during the past 12 months while in prison. The response categories included never, once, two to five times, six to twelve times, and over twelve times. Since the majority of the sample (i.e., 95 percent) reported no gang involvement in prison during the last year, it was feasible to recode never as no (i.e., coded as zero) and the other responses as yes (i.e., coded as one). Table 4.2 shows that the gang presence inside prisons in this sample is low. The average rate of gang involvement was about 5 percent. Inmates at nine prisons reported no gang involvement, while Southeastern Correctional Institution in Ohio had the highest rate of gang involvement with 17 percent of the subjects reporting involvement in gang activities during the past year.

The racial composition of each facility may be an influential cultural variable. Research suggests that minority inmates may be more likely than white prisoners to import values from the street culture. Collectively, this may make the prison a more threatening context. The percent nonwhite was computed by dividing the number of nonwhite inmates by the inmate population at each correctional facility. On average, 43 percent of inmates across these 30 prisons were nonwhite. The percent nonwhite was as high as 67 percent at Dayton Correctional Institution in Ohio and as low as 8 percent at Roederer Correctional Complex in Kentucky.

Young offenders may be more likely to import beliefs and attitudes from the street as well, and contribute to a more threatening prison culture. The percent under 25 year old was calculated by dividing the number of inmates under 25 by the inmate population at each correctional facility. The average percent of youthful offenders was around 18 percent across all prisons. Southeastern Tennessee State Regional Correctional Facility had the lowest rate of youthful offenders at 6 percent. About 51 percent of the inmates at Dayton Correctional Institution were under age 25, representing the highest rate of young prisoners.

The population at each facility was also included as a control variable because it may alter perceptions of crowding among inmates at the micro-level. Inmate populations ranged from 190 prisoners at Frankfort Career Development Center in Kentucky to 2,281 at Ross Correctional Institution in Ohio. The mean population across sampled prisons was 1,274 inmates at the time of the survey.

The inmate-to-staff ratio was also treated as a control variable in the present study. However, it may be that lower ratios of inmates to staff may signify a more controlled and custodial prison and thus contribute to feelings of deprivation (i.e., loss of autonomy, etc.). This variable was computed by dividing the number of inmates by the number of custodial staff at each correctional facility. On average, there are 5 inmates for every one custodial staff across all prisons. However, Noble Correctional Institution had 2 inmates for every staff. Bell County Forestry camp had the highest ratio with only 1 custodial staff member for every 8 prisoners.

A series of dummy variables was included in the multivariate models in order to discern the significance of the geographic location. Specifically, separate dummy variables were created for Kentucky, Tennessee, and Ohio. This was done primarily to test for any geographical effects on the dependent variables. These variables were included primarily as an exploratory exercise. At the state level, the mean of .367 for the Kentucky dummy variable indicates that about 37 percent of the prisons in this sample were located in Kentucky. The mean of .267 for the Tennessee dummy variable suggests that about 26 percent of the prisons in this sample were found in Tennessee. Lastly, the mean of .367 for the

Ohio dummy variable suggests that about 37 percent of the prisons in this sample were found in Ohio.

## Multilevel Hypotheses

Several general expectations guided this multilevel analysis of prisonization. First, the social processes of prisonization and misconduct should vary across prisons. Second, elements from both deprivation and importation theory should significantly affect prisonization and misconduct at both levels of analysis. Moreover, the effects of Level 1 independent variables on prisonization and misconduct should vary across contexts. Third, prisonization should be a significant predictor of general institutional misconduct. Fourth, Level 2 independent variables should have main effects on institutional processes such as prisonization and misconduct. Lastly, the contextual features of prisons should intensity the effects of individual-level social processes such as deprivation and importation on prisonization and misconduct. The more specific hypotheses are spelled out below.

Level 1 Hypotheses
1.  The mean level of prisonization will vary across prison contexts.
2.  The mean level of institutional misconduct will also vary across prisons.
3.  Older convicts will report higher degrees of prisonization. Specifically, as age increases so too will prisonization.
4.  Furthermore, the effect of age on prisonization will vary across prisons.
5.  Holding all other variables constant, nonwhite inmates will have a higher degree of prisonization than white inmates.
6.  Moreover, the effect of race on prisonization will vary across correctional facilities.
7.  Inmates with more extensive criminal backgrounds will be more prisonized. In particular, when controlling for all other variables, a convict's level of prisonization will increase as his prior incarcerations increase.
8.  Additionally, the effect of prior incarcerations on prisonization will vary across prisons.

9.  All else being equal, inmates who have served time for a prior violent crime will have a higher degree of prisonization than those inmates who have not served time for a violent offense.

10. Moreover, the effect of prior violence on prisonization will vary across prisons.

11. Convicts who experience many situational problems inside prison will have higher degrees of prisonization. That is, controlling for all other variables, an inmate's level of prisonization will increase as his situational problems increase.

12. Furthermore, the effect of situational problems on prisonization will vary across penitentiaries.

13. Inmates with longer sentences will be more highly prisonized. Specifically, all else being equal, an inmate's level of prisonization will increase as his sentence length increases.

14. Moreover, the effect of sentence length on prisonization will vary across prisons.

15. Inmates who have served more time will report higher degrees of prisonization. In particular, when controlling for all other factors, an inmate's prisonization score will increase as his time served increases.

16. Additionally, the effect of time served on prisonization will vary across contexts.

17. Convicts who receive fewer visits from family and friends will be more highly prisonized. Specifically, net all other effects, an inmate's level of prisonization will increase as the amount of visits from his family and friends decreases.

18. Furthermore, the effect of visits on prisonization will vary across prisons.

19. All else being equal, a convict's degree of prisonization will increase as the amount of letters from his family and friends decline.

20. Also, the effect of letters on prisonization will vary across prisons.

21. When controlling for all other variables, an inmate's level of prisonization will increase as the extent of his prison friendships increases.

22. Moreover, the effect of inmate friendships on prisonization will vary across prison contexts.

23. Inmates with friends inside prison who were formally charged or could have been formally charged with institutional misconduct will report higher degrees of prisonization. In particular, net all other effects, an inmate's level of prisonization will increase as the number of his deviant friends increases.
24. Furthermore, the effect of deviant friends on prisonization will vary across prisons.
25. Convicts who perceive that the correctional institution where they are housed is crowded will be more highly prisonized. Specifically, when controlling for all other variables, a convict's level of prisonization will increase as his perception of crowding increases.
26. Moreover, the effect of crowding on prisonization will vary across correctional facilities.
27. Level 1 control variables (i.e., self-esteem, definitions, coping difficulties, and religious involvement) will have no effects on the level of prisonization.
28. Inmates who report higher degrees of prisonization will engage in more acts of institutional misconduct. Specifically, net all other effects, an inmate's institutional misconduct will increase as his prisonization score increases.
29. Furthermore, the effect of prisonization on institutional misconduct will vary across correctional facilities.

Level 2 Hypotheses
1. When controlling for all other factors, as the age of the prison increases, inmates within these facilities will report increases in their levels of prisonization and institutional misconduct.
2. Holding all other variables constant, convicts in maximum security institutions will report higher degrees of prisonization and more acts of institutional misconduct.
3. Net all other effects, as the number of programs offered in a correctional facility increases, inmates within this institution will report lower levels of prisonization and institutional misconduct.
4. Controlling for all other variables, as crowding in prison increases, convicts within these facilities will report a higher levels of prisonization and misconduct.

5.  All else being equal, inmates will report higher levels of prisonization and misconduct in prisons with a pronounced gang presence.
6.  Net all other effects, as the amount of nonwhite inmates in prison increases, convicts will report increases in their levels of prisonization and misconduct.
7.  When controlling for all other variables, as the amount of inmates under age 25 increases, convicts will report higher levels of prisonization and misconduct.
8.  Level 2 control variables (i.e., population and inmate-to-staff ratio) will have no effects on the level of prisonization and misconduct.
9.  State-level effects will not be observed in this sample for either dependent variable.

Multilevel Interactions

The specification of contextual interactions in regard to the current project is an entirely exploratory matter. However, Woolredge et al. (2001) note that cross-level interactions do occur inside prison. As such, one very general multilevel hypothesis is appropriate:

1.  When controlling for all other factors, the Level 2 deprivation variables will intensify the effects of Level 1 independent variables on prisonization and institutional misconduct.

## A Review of the Hierarchical Modeling of Prisonization

A hierarchical model of prisonization should have, at a minimum, two levels. Inmates at Level 1 are nested within prisons at Level 2. Hierarchical linear modeling employs the use of sub-models to analyze hierarchically ordered data. Level 1 parameters can be estimated from Level 2 coefficients. First, statistical tests will determine if there is Level 2 variance in either prisonization or misconduct. This step is generally referred to as the null model. Then, the analysis will reveal variation in the effects of Level 1 independent variables across prisons (i.e., macro-level units). This step is called the random coefficients model. If either the intercepts or effects vary, then contextual predictors will be added to the model. Interactions between the individual-level and prison-level variables will then be used to determine the extent to which prison context influences the effects of micro-predictors on prisonization and misconduct. The last stage is often referred to as the contextual model.

# CHAPTER 5

# Preliminary Analyses of Correctional Context

Prison is a context that exerts a definite influence over the social relations of those who enter its domain. However, this influence varies from one institution to another. The features of prisons also vary from one facility to the next and from state to state. This contextual analysis of prison life is actually based on the assumption that there is significant heterogeneity between correctional facilities. In this chapter, the differences and similarities between correctional institutions in Kentucky, Tennessee, and Ohio are presented. First, the origin of the corrections in each state is reviewed. The thirty prisons under investigation in the current project are identified and described. Next, the differences among the thirty prisons and between the three states are elaborated. The variables that constitute the conceptual model are broken down by state and by institution. Analyses of variance reveal mean differences in the Level 1 and Level 2 variables across three states and thirty prisons. Finally, several measures from the each state's Department of Correction are contrasted with aggregated survey responses to elucidate potential biases.

## The Origins of Corrections Across Three States

Although the origins of corrections in Kentucky, Tennessee, and Ohio were distinct historical events, all three beginnings share certain similarities. Correctional policies in these states began almost immediately after their entry into the Union. For example, Kentucky became a state in 1792. At that time, death by hanging was the punishment for every felony except one. The penalty for attempted rape of a white woman by a black man was castration. In 1799, Kentucky State Penitentiary (KSP) was erected in Frankfort. It was the first penitentiary built west of the Allegheny Mountains. Tennessee entered the Union in 1796 and enacted legislation that provided the death penalty for horse stealing. In 1831, Tennessee State Penitentiary (TSP) became operational in Nashville. Ohio became a state in 1803 and the Ohio State Penitentiary (OSP) was constructed in 1835. Capital punishment, consisting of death by hanging, was practiced in Ohio as early as 1803. Thus, each state in this analysis became part of the United States around the start of the nineteenth century and shortly thereafter erected a state penitentiary. Penal policy was a primary concern of the newly formed state legislatures, and all three states practiced capital punishment during this time period.

The conditions of imprisonment were also quite similar among the three state penitentiaries (i.e., Kentucky State Penitentiary, Tennessee State Penitentiary, and Ohio State Penitentiary) during the nineteenth century. Punishment was the primary function of the early correctional systems. All three states enacted legislation regarding capital punishment shortly after their admittance to the Union. According to the Ohio Department of Rehabilitation and Correction (2001), the electric chair was introduced in 1897 at Ohio State Penitentiary to replace death by hanging. The electric chair in Ohio was designed by Charles Justice, a convict imprisoned for robbery and burglary. In an unfortunate twist of fate, Justice was convicted of a murder charge after he was released for serving his initial sentence for theft. He was sentenced to death, and electrocuted in the device that he helped to build (Ohio Department of Rehabilitation and Correction, 2001). The first man was electrocuted in Tennessee during 1915. Kentucky holds the record for the most men electrocuted in one day when seven men were put to death in the electric chair in one night in 1929. However, all sampled states currently use lethal injection as the primary method of capital punishment. Nowadays, the death sentence is carried out at Kentucky State Penitentiary located in Eddyville, Riverbend Maximum Security Institution in Nashville, and Southern Ohio Correctional Facility in Lucasville.

Corporal punishment was also frequently used to subdue prisoners and make them comply with administration. Inmates were often whipped with a leather strap 18 inches long, 2 inches wide, and attached to a wooden handle (Kentucky Department of Correction, 2001). The strap was often soaked in water and dragged through sand before it was used. In 1894, a survey of state correctional facilities revealed that Kentucky used lashing 300 times more often than any other state (Kentucky Department of Corrections, 2001). Other methods of punishment included solitary confinement on bread and water, deprivation of light and air, hanging by chains, the ball and chain, and the thumb stall. Corporal punishment was often severe and sometimes resulted in death. Corporal punishment persisted until as late as 1966 when it was finally abolished for adult offenders (Tennessee Department of Correction, 2001).

Hard labor was another common feature of prison life during the 1800s. In particular, the penitentiaries and inmates were often leased to private businessmen for a return of a percentage of the profits from labor. According to the Tennessee Department of Correction (2001), the convict leasing system in Tennessee began in 1870 and was the first true work release program in the country. Inmates worked in hemp factories, chair making, shoe making, cooperage, wagon making, sleigh making, weaving, mining, farming, and construction of governmental buildings, railroads, highways, personal houses, and other structures.

The Kentucky Department of Correction (2001) published excerpts from the journal of Louis Curry who served as warden of the Kentucky Branch Penitentiary at Eddyville. One such entry presents a vivid account of punishment and labor as follows:

> Prisoner Berry, #289, was put on report for refusing to haul stone through the sally port gate. He said he was not a beast of burden and does not care if the prison wall ever gets finished. Beast of burden, indeed! I ordered him confined and chained to the dungeon cell beneath two-block. Eventually, I predict, Berry will learn to march to my tune. There is yet one-third of the wall to be built. And, every able-bodied prisoner will be expected to do his share (Curry, 1889/2001).

Another incident where punishment mixed with labor to produce a deadly result occurred when two inmates who had been assigned to dig a water works reservoir in Lexington were beaten to death by the contractors overseeing the project. In Kentucky, the warden system replaced the lessee system in 1880. Forced labor remained a central feature of early correctional systems.

In addition to punishment and hard labor, illness and disease were rampant in the early prison systems. In 1833, all but two inmates in Kentucky had cholera. Pneumonia was common. From 1878 to 1879, one hundred six inmates in Kentucky died of diseases such as scurvy. Likewise the Kentucky Department of Correction (2001) reports that, from 1891 to

1892, 48 percent of inmate deaths at two prisons in Kentucky were due to tuberculosis. Typhoid fever broke out at the Kentucky State Penitentiary in Eddyville during 1913. The outbreak of these diseases in correctional facilities was often attributed to overcrowded conditions. In the 1800s, it was common for three or four convicts to be housed in one cell (Kentucky Department of Correction, 2001).

In sum, corrections in Kentucky, Tennessee, and Ohio originated as distinct historical events but developed quite similarly during the nineteenth century. Correctional policies were enacted almost immediately after the states became part of the U.S. Furthermore, penitentiaries were among the first state enterprises. The conditions of imprisonment in these early penitentiaries were similar and consisted of capital and corporal punishment, brutality, hard labor, crowded conditions, and widespread disease. The early correctional system in Kentucky was particularly arbitrary and capricious. According to the Kentucky Department of Correction (2001), in 1880 the Kentucky Senate established new prison rules that described plainly each offense, the penalty, and the method of punishment. In fact, at one point, the rules of Ohio State Penitentiary were ordered into effect at Kentucky State Penitentiary by the Kentucky senate.

## The Features of Corrections Across Three States

Thirty prisons are under investigation in the present study: eleven from Kentucky, eight from Tennessee, and eleven from Ohio. Table 5.1 displays the number of surveyed inmates in each prison as well as the acronyms used to abbreviate the names of each institution. Collectively, there are fourteen state adult institutions located in the state of Kentucky. The eleven institutions in this sample included Bell County Forestry Camp, Blackburn Correctional Complex, Eastern Kentucky Correctional Complex, Frankfort Career Development Center, Green River Correctional Complex, Kentucky State Reformatory, Luther Luckett Correctional Complex, Northpoint Training Center, Roederer Correctional Complex, and Western Kentucky Correctional Complex.

Table 5.1
Sample Size and Acronyms for Prisons

| Prison | Acronym | Sample Size |
|---|---|---|
| *Kentucky* | | |
| Bell County Forestry Camp | BCFC | 28 |
| Blackburn Correctional Complex | BCC | 51 |
| Eastern Kentucky Correctional Complex | EKCC | 54 |
| Frankfort Career Development Center | FCDC | 22 |
| Green River Correctional Complex | GRCC | 76 |
| Kentucky State Penitentiary | KSP | 20 |
| Kentucky State Reformatory | KSR | 34 |
| Luther Luckett Correctional Complex | LLCC | 19 |
| Northpoint Training Center | NTC | 36 |
| Roederer Correctional Complex | RCC | 27 |
| Western Kentucky Correctional Complex | WKCC | 21 |
| *Tennessee* | | |
| Middle Tennessee Correctional Complex | MTCC | 21 |
| Morgan County Correctional Complex | MCCC | 66 |
| Riverbend Maximum Security Institution | RMSI | 20 |
| Northeast Correctional Complex | NECC | 33 |
| Northwest Correctional Complex | NWCC | 62 |
| South Central Correctional Facility | SCCF | 37 |
| Southeastern Tennessee State Regional Correctional Facility | STSRCF | 35 |
| Turney Correctional Industrial Prison and Farm | TCIPF | 26 |
| *Ohio* | | |
| Chillicothe Correctional Institution | CCI | 46 |
| Dayton Correctional Institution | DCI | 10 |
| London Correctional Institution | LCI | 46 |
| Madison Correctional Institution | MCI | 12 |
| Noble Correctional Institution | NCI | 53 |
| Orient Correctional Institution | OCI | 26 |
| Pickaway Correctional Institution | PCI | 16 |
| Ross Correctional Institution | RCI | 50 |
| Southeastern Correctional Institution | SCI | 29 |
| Southern Ohio Correctional Facility | SOCF | 41 |
| Warren Correctional Institution | WCI | 37 |

Three adult institutions (i.e., Lee Adjustment Center, Marion Adjustment Center, and Kentucky Correctional Institution for Women) in Kentucky were excluded from the sample. The Corrections Corporation of America (CCA) owns and operates Lee Adjustment Center and Marion Adjustment Center. The Commonwealth contracts services through CCA. In sum, almost 80 percent of Kentucky's adult correctional institutions were included in the final Level 2 sample of prisons.

In 1997, the number of state prisons in Tennessee was reduced from twenty to fourteen. Several institutions that were in close proximity to one another were merged while another four were simply closed. Fourteen correctional facilities now comprise the state prison system in Tennessee. The eight prisons from Tennessee that were under investigation in this project included Middle Tennessee Correctional Complex, Morgan County Correctional Complex (i.e., part of Brushy Mountain Correctional Complex), Riverbend Maximum Security Institution, Northeast Correctional Complex, Northwest Correctional Complex, South Central Correctional Complex, Southeastern Tennessee State Regional Correctional Facility, and Turney Center Industrial Prison and Farm. The six prisons from Tennessee that were excluded in this sample were West Tennessee State Penitentiary, Wayne County Boot Camp, Tennessee Prison for Women, Mark H. Luttrell Correctional Center, Hardeman County Correctional Center, and Lois M. Deberry Special Needs Facility. Thus, 57 percent of the adult prisons in Tennessee were included in the final sample at Level 2.

Thirty-four correctional facilities comprise the Ohio state prison system. Eleven of these were included in the present study: Chillicothe Correctional Institution, Dayton Correctional Institution, London Correctional Institution, Madison Correctional Institution, Noble Correctional Institution, Orient Correctional Institution, Pickaway Correctional Institution, Ross Correctional Institution, Southeastern Correctional Institution, Southern Ohio Correctional Facility, and Warren Correctional Institution. Twenty-three institutions in Ohio were excluded from the present study. These include Allen Correctional Institution, Belmont Correctional Institution, Corrections Medical Center, Correctional Reception Center, Franklin Pre-Release Center, Grafton Correctional Institution, Hocking Correctional Facility, Lake Erie Correctional Institution, Lebanon Correctional Institution, Lima

Correctional Institution, Lorain Correctional Institution, Mansfield Correctional Institution, Marion Correctional Institution, Montgomery Education and Pre-Release Center, North Central Correctional Institution, North Coast Correctional Treatment Facility, Northeast Pre-Release Center, Oakwood Correctional Facility, Ohio Reformatory for Women, Ohio State Penitentiary, Richland Correctional Institution, Toledo Correctional Institution, and Trumbull Correctional Institution. In sum, 32 percent of the correctional facilities in Ohio made it into the final sample of prisons at Level 2.

## Level 2 Variables Within and Between Three States

Correctional facilities may be differentiated according to structural and organizational features such as age, security level, programming, crowding, gang presence, percent nonwhite, percent under 25 years old, total inmate population, and inmate-to-staff ratio. These Level 2 variables are measured at the macro-level of analysis. Data on all but one (i.e., gang presence) of these items were obtained from official sources at each state's Department of Correction. The characteristics of sampled correctional facilities across Kentucky, Tennessee, and Ohio are displayed in Table 5.2. This visual presentation allows for quick comparisons of prisons within and between states. In this section, the structural and organization differences within the state prisons are revealed. The state correctional facilities are further differentiated by comparing the mean values on these Level 2 variables between states.

### Prisons in Kentucky: Level 2

Prisons in Kentucky vary in their structural and cultural features. For instance, the Green River Correctional Complex, located in the western part of the state, was the newest facility in the Kentucky sample of prisons at the time of this study. As previously mentioned, the Kentucky State

Table 5.2
Characteristics of Prisons: Level 2 Variables ($n_j$=30)

| Prison | Age of Prison | Security Level | Number of Programs | Population/ Capacity | Gang Presence |
|---|---|---|---|---|---|
| *KY* | | | | | |
| BCFC | 39 | minimum | 2 | .95 | .04 |
| BCC | 29 | minimum | 7 | .99 | .06 |
| EKCC | 11 | medium | 8 | 1.00 | .04 |
| FCDC | 25 | minimum | 2 | .93 | .00 |
| GRCC | 7 | medium | 7 | 1.02 | .04 |
| KSP | 117 | maximum | 5 | 1.00 | .15 |
| KSR | 64 | medium | 15 | 1.00 | .03 |
| LLCC | 20 | medium | 7 | 1.00 | .05 |
| NTC | 18 | medium | 6 | 1.00 | .11 |
| RCC | 25 | medium | 3 | 1.02 | .00 |
| WKCC | 34 | medium | 4 | .98 | .00 |
| *TN* | | | | | |
| MTCC | 22 | close | 5 | .89 | .00 |
| MCCC | 12 | minimum | 6 | 1.00 | .03 |
| RMSI | 12 | maximum | 4 | .96 | .00 |
| NECC | 10 | maximum | 11 | 1.04 | .09 |
| NWCC | 9 | close | 18 | .97 | .10 |
| SCCF | 9 | close | 10 | 1.00 | .08 |
| STSRCF | 21 | medium | 6 | .94 | .03 |
| TCIPF | 30 | close | 10 | 1.01 | .12 |
| *OH* | | | | | |
| CCI | 35 | medium | 10 | 1.31 | .00 |
| DCI | 28 | medium | 6 | .96 | .00 |
| LCI | 77 | mixed | 17 | .83 | .02 |
| MCI | 14 | mixed | 7 | .94 | .00 |
| NCI | 5 | medium | 15 | 1.03 | .04 |
| OCI | 17 | medium | 11 | 1.07 | .04 |
| PCI | 17 | minimum | 8 | .91 | .00 |
| RCI | 14 | mixed | 11 | 1.39 | .08 |
| SCI | 21 | mixed | 9 | .91 | .17 |
| SOCF | 29 | maximum | 4 | .88 | .10 |
| WCI | 12 | close | 6 | 1.06 | .03 |

Table 5.2 (continued)
Characteristics of Prisons: Level 2 Variables ($n_j$=30)

| Prison | Percent Nonwhite | Percent Under 25 | Inmate Population | Inmate to Staff Ratio |
|---|---|---|---|---|
| *KY* | | | | |
| BCFC | .27 | .26 | 218 | 8.72 |
| BCC | .36 | .11 | 392 | 5.52 |
| EKCC | .35 | .25 | 1621 | 5.83 |
| FCDC | .47 | .09 | 190 | 7.04 |
| GRCC | .34 | .19 | 917 | 5.15 |
| KSP | .30 | .21 | 815 | 3.05 |
| KSR | .26 | .12 | 1554 | 4.10 |
| LLCC | .31 | .15 | 975 | 5.36 |
| NTC | .47 | .26 | 1097 | 5.27 |
| RCC | .08 | .06 | 796 | 4.82 |
| WKCC | .32 | .15 | 565 | 4.63 |
| *TN* | | | | |
| MTCC | .58 | .15 | 943 | 3.51 |
| MCCC | .27 | .10 | 1589 | 4.38 |
| RMSI | .52 | .09 | 651 | 2.77 |
| NECC | .27 | .07 | 1656 | 5.26 |
| NWCC | .65 | .23 | 2144 | 5.76 |
| SCCF | .53 | .10 | 1513 | 5.77 |
| STSRCF | .41 | .06 | 919 | 4.60 |
| TCIPF | .54 | .10 | 1124 | 5.85 |
| *OH* | | | | |
| CCI | .40 | .10 | 2199 | 5.86 |
| DCI | .67 | .51 | 480 | 3.97 |
| LCI | .49 | .18 | 1876 | 6.68 |
| MCI | .40 | .19 | 2060 | 6.19 |
| NCI | .41 | .18 | 1904 | 2.08 |
| OCI | .55 | .11 | 1948 | 5.76 |
| PCI | .51 | .20 | 1700 | 7.14 |
| RCI | .52 | .22 | 2281 | 5.73 |
| SCI | .52 | .44 | 1361 | 4.79 |
| SOCF | .62 | .16 | 1442 | 2.66 |
| WCI | .48 | .21 | 1279 | 5.04 |

Penitentiary was the oldest prison in the Kentucky sample. It, too, is located in the western part of Kentucky. The average age of sampled prisons in Kentucky was 35.36 years. In addition, three minimum, seven medium, and one maximum institution from Kentucky were included in the sample. Both Bell County Forestry Camp and Frankfort Career Development Center had the fewest number (i.e., 2 each) of educational and vocational programs in the Kentucky sample. Kentucky State Reformatory had the most programs with a combined number of 15. The average number of educational and vocational programs for sampled Kentucky prisons was 6.

Likewise, sampled institutions in Kentucky were, on average, filled to 99 percent of their capacity. Frankfort Career Development Center was at 92 percent operating capacity, while three institutions were operating at above 100 percent at the time of this study. Furthermore, the rate of gang involvement in Kentucky's sampled prisons ranged from a low of 0 percent at three facilities to a high of 15 percent at Kentucky State Penitentiary. On average, 5 percent of subjects in Kentucky's sampled prisons had engaged in gang activities inside prison within the past year. The prison-level percentage of nonwhite inmates ranged from 8 percent at Roederer to 47 percent at both Frankfort Career Development Center and Northpoint Training Center. The average prison-level percent nonwhite across sampled Kentucky prisons was 32 percent. The mean rate of inmates under 25 years old was 17 percent in Kentucky. The lowest proportion (i.e., 6 percent) of under 25 was located at Roederer Correctional Complex. Northpoint Training Center had the highest rate of inmates under 25 years old at 26 percent. Total inmate populations ranged from 190 at Frankfort Career Development Center to 1621 at Eastern Kentucky Correctional Complex. The average inmate population for prisons sampled in Kentucky was 831. Lastly, at the Kentucky State Penitentiary, there was one staff member for every three inmates. However, at Bell County Forestry Camp, for every 8 inmates there was only one custodial staff member.

Prisons in Tennessee: Level 2

A number of Level 2 characteristics also varied among correctional institutions in Tennessee. In this sample, both Northwest Correctional Complex and South Central Correctional Facility were the newest prisons.

South Central Correctional Facility is owned by the State of Tennessee but managed by Corrections Corporation of America. The average age for prisons in the Tennessee sample was 16.75 years. The oldest sampled prison in Tennessee was Turney Center Industrial Prison and Farm in Only, Tennessee. Furthermore, one minimum, one medium, two maximum, and four close security correctional facilities in Tennessee were included in the overall sample. In the Tennessee sample, Riverbend Maximum Security Institution had the fewest number (i.e., 4) of educational and vocational programs while Northwest Correctional Complex had the greatest amount (i.e., 18). The mean number of programs in sampled Tennessee prisons was 9.13. Additionally, on average, sampled correctional facilities in the state were operating at 98 percent of their capacity at the time of this study. In fact, Middle Tennessee Correctional Complex was operating at 89 percent of capacity while Northeast Correctional Complex was operating at 104 percent of capacity. The age of the institution, its security level, the number of vocational programs, and its degree of crowding are all qualities of institutional living that are consistent with deprivation theory.

Other institutional features have a more imported nature. For instance, the rate of gang involvement among surveyed prisoners in sampled Tennessee institutions varied from 0 percent at both Middle Tennessee Correctional Complex and Riverbend Maximum Security Institution to 12 percent at Turney Center Industrial Prison and Farm. On average, about 6 percent of prisoners in sampled correctional facilities throughout Tennessee reported gang activity inside prison within the past twelve months. Furthermore, the mean rate of nonwhite inmates in the Tennessee sample was around 47 percent with Northwest Correctional Complex reporting the highest percentage of nonwhite convicts with 65 percent. The nonwhite inmate populations at both Morgan County Correctional Complex and Northeast Correctional Complex were around 27 percent, the lowest in this sample of Tennessee prisons. Moreover, Northwest Correctional Complex also had the highest percentage (i.e., 27 percent) of prisoners under age 25 in the Tennessee sample. The average rate of inmates under 25 years old was around 11 percent in this sample. For the Tennessee sample, Southeastern TN State Regional Correctional Facility reported the lowest rate of youthful inmates with only 6 percent.

Related organizational characteristics include a prison's total inmate population and its inmate-to-staff ratio. Northwest Correctional Complex also had a total of 2,144 or the largest prisoner population in this sample of facilities in Tennessee. The average inmate population in this state sample was around 1,317 individuals. In the Tennessee sample, Riverbend Maximum Security Institution housed the fewest inmates with only 651 men incarcerated at the time of this study. Finally, Riverbend also had the lowest inmate-to-staff ratio in the sample with one custodial officer for every 2.77 inmates. At Turney Center Industrial Prison and Farm, there were 5.85 inmates for every one officer. The mean inmate-to-staff ratio for sampled prisons in Tennessee was 4.74.

Prisons in Ohio: Level 2

The organizational, cultural, and structural features of prisons within Ohio varied just as they did within Kentucky and Tennessee. First off, the mean age for sampled institutions in Ohio was 25.93 years. Noble Correctional Institution was the newest facility in the Ohio sample and has only been operational for five years. London Correctional Institution was the oldest in this sample at 77 years. Included in the final sample were one minimum, four medium, four mixed, one close, and one maximum security institution from Ohio. In the Ohio sample, Southern Ohio Correctional Facility offered the fewest programs (i.e., 4), but London Correctional Institution had as many as 17 educational and vocational programs in house. The average number of programs in this sample of Ohio's prisons was around 9.45. Furthermore, the most crowded institutions throughout the entire sample appeared in Ohio, with Ross Correctional Institution operating at 139 percent of its capacity. London Correctional Institution had the lowest degree of crowding among sampled prisons in Ohio, operating at only 83 percent of capacity. On average, sampled institutions within Ohio were operating at around 103 percent of their capacity.

Institutional features are often determined by the characteristics that inmates import from outside prison. In particular, a prison-level average of 4 percent of inmates reported gang activity across sampled prisons within Ohio. Sampled inmates in three institutions reported no gang involvement, while the highest rate of prior gang involvement inside prison occurred in Southeastern Correctional Institution with 17 percent of sampled prisoners reporting gang activity. Additionally, Southern Ohio

Correctional Facility had the highest percentage of nonwhite inmates (i.e., 62 percent) in the sampled prisons within Ohio. The average rate of nonwhite inmates in the Ohio sample was around 51 percent. Two institutions (i.e., Chillicothe Correctional Institution and Madison Correctional Institution) had about 40 percent nonwhite inmates, the lowest in sampled facilities across Ohio. Chillicothe Correctional Institution also had the lowest rate of inmates under 25 years old. Dayton Correctional Institution had the highest percentage (i.e., 51 percent) of youthful convicts. The average prison-level percent under 25 years old was 23 percent across the 11 sampled Ohio prisons.

The total inmate population and the inmate-to-staff ratio round out the organizational features of prisons under examination in the current project. In the Ohio sample, Ross Correctional Institution had the greatest inmate population of 2,199 convicts. Dayton Correctional Institution housed 480 prisoners, the lowest population among sampled facilities within Ohio. The mean inmate population for sampled institutions in Ohio was 1685 at the time of this study. Lastly, on average, there were 5 inmates to every one custodial officer in Ohio. In this sample, Noble Correctional Institution had the lowest inmate-to-staff ratio with 2.08 convicts for every one custodial officer, and Pickaway Correctional Institution had the highest inmate-to-staff ratio with one officer for every 7.14 inmates.

## Level 2 Variables Between Three States

A casual glance at Table 5.2 and Table 5.3 suggests that there are differences in the mean levels of institutional characteristics among the Kentucky, Tennessee, and Ohio samples of prisons. Table 5.3 shows the descriptive statistics for prisons in this tri-state region and reveals the mean level of each Level 2 variable by state. For example, the average age of sampled correctional facilities in Kentucky was 35.36 years. The mean age of sampled prisons in Tennessee was only 16.75 years. The mean inmate-to-staff ratio in Kentucky was also the highest among the three

Table 5.3

Means and Standard Deviations (S.D.) for Level 2 Variables by State

| Variable | *Kentucky* | | *Tennessee* | | *Ohio* | |
|---|---|---|---|---|---|---|
| | Mean | S.D. | Mean | S.D. | Mean | S.D. |
| Age of Prison | 35.36 | 31.13 | 16.75 | 7.81 | 25.93 | 23.28 |
| Security Level | .09 | .30 | .25 | .46 | .09 | .30 |
| Programs | 6.00 | 3.66 | 9.13 | 4.42 | 9.45 | 3.93 |
| Crowding | .99 | .03 | .98 | .05 | 1.03 | .18 |
| Gang Presence | .05 | .05 | .06 | .06 | .04 | .06 |
| Percent Nonwhite | .32 | .11 | .47 | .14 | .51 | .09 |
| Percent Under 25 Years | .17 | .08 | .11 | .06 | .23 | .13 |
| Population | 831 | 479 | 1317 | 491 | 1685 | 519 |
| Inmates to Staff | 5.41 | 1.49 | 4.74 | 1.15 | 5.08 | 1.60 |

state samples with 5.41 inmates for every one custodial officer. On average, Tennessee had a greater gang presence than the other states with an average of 6 percent of inmates reporting some gang involvement in the past year. Additionally, the mean levels of certain characteristics were higher in the Ohio sample than the other states. For instance, Ohio had the highest mean level of programming with 9.45 combined educational and vocational programs. Ohio was also operating at, on average, 103 percent of capacity, the greatest crowding ratio among the three states. The mean rate of nonwhite inmates (i.e., 51 percent) was also higher in Ohio with 51 percent nonwhite. Ohio also had the greatest mean rate of inmates under age 25 years old. Lastly, the average inmate population was higher at 1685 in Ohio than the other two state samples.

Although the mean levels of institutional features do not appear equal across the three states, an analytical technique known as analysis of variance (ANOVA) was used to determine if these differences were statistically significant. ANOVAs were ran on all continuous, prison-level variables (i.e., age of prison, programs, crowding, gang presence, percent nonwhite, percent under 25, population, and inmate-to-staff ratio) in the conceptual model. Significant F ratios were obtained for three of the eight variables. The null hypothesis held that the means between all three states are the same for prison age, programming, crowding, gang presence, and inmate-to-staff ratio. That is, the F statistics were non-significant for these variables. However, for sampled institutions, a statistically significant (i.e., at the .001 level) F ratio of 8.806 was obtained for the variable percent nonwhite. This indicated that the mean levels of the percentage of nonwhite inmates among the three states were not equal. A multiple comparison procedure, known as the Bonferroni test, revealed significant differences between Kentucky's mean percent nonwhite and both Tennessee's and Ohio's mean levels of percent nonwhite. In particular, the average percentage of nonwhite inmates in Kentucky's sampled prisons was significantly less than either Tennessee's mean percent nonwhite or Ohio's mean level.

Furthermore, an analysis of variance revealed that the mean levels of the percentage of inmates under 25 years old were not equal across Kentucky, Tennessee, and Ohio. In particular, a significant (i.e., at the .05 level) F statistic of 3.448 was obtained. Bonferroni procedures determined that Tennessee's percent under 25 years old was significantly less than Ohio's rate of young prisoners. The final significant analysis of variance concerned the inmate population. The statistically significant (i.e., at the .05 level) F ratio of 8.139 suggested that the average inmate populations were not equal among the three states. Specifically, multiple comparison tests revealed that the mean population in Kentucky was significantly less than the average population in Ohio.

**Level 1 Variables Within and Between Three States**

The micro, individual-level variables that constitute Level 1 of the conceptual model represent the characteristics of prisoners within the various state penitentiaries. Nineteen variables are measured at this level of analysis and include information on inmates such as their degree of prisonization, rule violations, age, race, prior incarcerations, etc. Level 1 data came from the surveys that were administered to prisoners. The information obtained from these questionnaires also describe the samples of inmates at each prison. For example, the youngest subjects in the final sample were 18 years old. They were incarcerated at Northwest Correctional Complex in Tennessee and Pickaway Correction Institution in Ohio. However, on average, the youngest group of inmates to take part in this project was from Dayton Correctional Institution which had the lowest mean respondent age across the different prisons of 23.80 years.

In addition to the structural and organizational features that differentiate prisons, the sample characteristics at each facility also distinguish correctional contexts. Table 5.4 illustrates the descriptive statistics for Level 1 variables by state. In this section, the sample characteristics within state correctional institutions are described. The state prisons are further described by comparing their means on the Level 1 variables.

Prisons in Kentucky: Level 1

The sample characteristics of correctional facilities varied within Kentucky. Prisonization, an outcome variable in the conceptual model, was lowest at Luther Luckett Correctional Complex and highest at Kentucky State Penitentiary. The average score on the prisonization scale across sampled institutions in Kentucky was 40.07. Inmate subjects also reported the largest number of rule violations at Kentucky State Penitentiary. On average, respondents at that facility were issued 3.15 tickets for institutional misconduct over a twelve month period. Subjects at Western Kentucky Correctional Complex reported the least average rule violations with only .05 write-ups for the same time frame. The average number of rule violations across sampled prisons in Kentucky was 1.08.

Table 5.4

Means and Standard Deviations (S.D.) for Level 1 Variables by State

| Variable | Kentucky | | Tennessee | | Ohio | |
|---|---|---|---|---|---|---|
| | Mean | S.D. | Mean | S.D. | Mean | S.D. |
| Prisonization | 40.07 | 10.41 | 41.64 | 11.47 | 40.06 | 9.74 |
| Rule Violations | 1.08 | 2.63 | 1.82 | 3.97 | 1.90 | 3.77 |
| Prisoner Age | 36.22 | 10.13 | 35.71 | 9.57 | 35.70 | 10.26 |
| Race | .38 | .49 | .47 | .50 | .47 | .50 |
| Prior Incarcerations | 2.99 | 4.98 | 2.18 | 2.92 | 1.12 | 2.71 |
| Prior Violence | .22 | .41 | .36 | .48 | .22 | .42 |
| Gang Involvement | .11 | .32 | .11 | .31 | .13 | .34 |
| Situational Problems | 37.54 | 9.66 | 38.00 | 9.91 | 37.99 | 9.22 |
| Sentence | 20.98 | 20.46 | 30.58 | 29.16 | 18.76 | 20.95 |
| Time Served | 6.10 | 4.91 | 8.53 | 6.66 | 7.66 | 6.10 |
| Visits | 2.92 | 1.58 | 2.60 | 1.55 | 2.66 | 1.55 |
| Letters | 4.48 | 1.02 | 4.23 | 1.20 | 4.31 | 1.13 |
| Prison Friends | 1.45 | .98 | 1.58 | 1.05 | 1.54 | .94 |
| Deviant Friends | 1.08 | 1.73 | 1.35 | 1.93 | .90 | 1.62 |
| Crowding | 1.67 | 1.04 | 2.28 | .91 | 2.01 | 1.01 |
| Self-esteem | 46.86 | 9.30 | 46.71 | 10.00 | 47.62 | 9.43 |
| Definitions | 12.89 | 3.69 | 12.68 | 3.53 | 12.61 | 3.47 |
| Copying Difficulty | 16.50 | 6.27 | 17.15 | 6.02 | 16.79 | 6.33 |
| Religious Involvement | .51 | .50 | .47 | .50 | .46 | .50 |

Independent variables from the importation model include age, race, prior incarcerations, prior violence, and prior gang involvement. Inmates at Kentucky State Reformatory were generally the oldest group sampled throughout this state. The average age of subjects from Kentucky was 36.22 years with the highest mean age of 42.25 years reported at Kentucky State Reformatory. Bell County Forestry Camp had the lowest mean age of surveyed prisoners at 32.14 years. Roederer Correctional Complex had 52 percent nonwhite subjects, the highest mean rate across the Kentucky sample. Kentucky State Reformatory had the lowest percentage of nonwhite research subjects (i.e., 12 percent). On average, 38 percent of respondents across Kentucky were nonwhite. Inmate subjects at Luther Luckett Correctional Complex reported the fewest prior adult incarcerations (i.e., 1.42) across Kentucky sampled correctional facilities. Subjects at Blackburn Correctional Complex had the greatest average number of prior incarceration at 5.01. On average, surveyed prisoners throughout the state reported almost 3 prior adult incarcerations.

The average rate of prior violent incarcerations for the Kentucky sample ranged from a low of 14 percent at Bell County Forestry Camp to a high of 35 percent at Kentucky State Penitentiary. The mean rate of inmate prior violence across sampled prisons within Kentucky was around 22 percent. Lastly, participants at Roederer Correctional Complex reported the lowest mean rate of prior gang involvement in the last year before incarceration at 4 percent. Subjects at Kentucky State Penitentiary had the highest rate of prior gang activities of 25 percent. On average, about 11 percent of surveyed prisoners throughout the Kentucky prison sample disclosed prior gang involvement on the street.

Deprivation variables include the extent of situational problems, sentence length, the amount of time served, the number of visits and letters from family and friends, the extensiveness of prison friendships, the number of deviant friends inside prison, and an inmate's perception of crowding. In Kentucky, the averages on the situational problems index ranged from a low of 34.38 at Western Kentucky Correctional Complex to a high of 39.19 at Bell County Forestry Camp. The mean for the entire sample was 37.54. Also, inmate subjects throughout the Kentucky sample were serving an average sentence of almost 21 years with a low of 10.63 years at Roederer Correctional Complex and a high of 37.89 years at Frankfort Career Development Center. On average, respondents across the state sample reported that they had already served about 6 years on this sentence. Again, subjects at Roederer had served the least average number of years with 3.61, while participants at Kentucky State Penitentiary had the greatest mean length of 9.56 years time served.

Social relationships were examined by two variables that tapped the degree of outside contacts and two variables that tapped the extensiveness of prison associations. The average number of visits from family and friends ranged from a low of 2.05 at Kentucky State Penitentiary to a high of 3.47 at Blackburn Correctional Complex. Across Kentucky sampled prisons, the mean number of visits from family and friends was almost 3 which indicated that inmates received, on average, three to six visits in the past year. Inmate subjects received more letters than visits. The mean number of letters received by participants across Kentucky was 4.48, indicating that inmates received well over six letters in the past year. In fact, on average, inmates in all but one institution reported receiving over six letters. Subjects at Kentucky State Reformatory reported receiving the fewest letters, somewhere between three and six. Furthermore, on average, respondents in Kentucky developed at least one and as many as five friendships inside prison. Of these institutional associations, at least one of these friends had done something for which they were formally charged or could have been charged. Sampled prisoners at Eastern Kentucky Correctional Complex reported the fewest mean number of deviant prison friends while inmate subjects at Green River Correctional Complex disclosed the highest number of deviant inmate buddies.

An inmate's perception of crowding rounds out the variables from the deprivation model that were tested in the current project. On average, sampled inmates throughout Kentucky felt somewhere between slightly and moderately crowded. Subjects at Luther Luckett Correctional Complex reported the highest mean perception of crowding, somewhere between moderately and extremely crowded. According to the surveyed prisoners, Frankfort Career Development Center felt the least crowded.

In addition to the importation and deprivation variables, several control variables were included in the study as well. Three of these controls (i.e., self-esteem, definitions toward the rules, and coping difficulties) are indices that were not very revealing. However, the extent of religious involvement in prison during the last twelve months is quite interesting. On average, about 51 percent of surveyed inmates in Kentucky reported attending religious services while in prison. The range of mean religious participation was wide. Roughly 89 percent of subjects at Luther Luckett Correctional Complex reported involvement in religious services, while only 26 percent of respondents at Roederer Correctional Complex were involved with religious activities in prison.

## Prisons in Tennessee: Level 1

Level 1 characteristics also fluctuated across sampled prisons in

Tennessee. The extent of prisonization throughout the Tennessee sample was lowest at Middle Tennessee Correctional Complex and highest at Northeast Correctional Complex. For the entire state sample, the mean score on the prisonization index was 41.64. Additionally, the measure of institutional misconduct ranged from a low of .05 mean rule violations at Middle Tennessee Correctional Complex to a high of 3.53 infractions at Northwest Correctional Complex. On average, sampled inmates in Tennessee received 1.82 tickets or rule violations within the past twelve months while in prison.

The mean levels of the importation variables were also calculated for the surveyed inmates within correctional facilities in Tennessee. On average, inmates were older at Riverbend Maximum Security Institution and younger at Northwest Correctional Complex. The mean age of sampled prisoners across Tennessee was 35.71 years. Northwest Correctional Complex also had the highest percent nonwhite subjects at 74 percent. Two institutions (i.e., Middle Tennessee Correctional Complex and Northeast Correctional Complex) had 21 percent nonwhite participants, the lowest rate across Tennessee. The mean percent of nonwhite inmate subjects across the entire state was around 47 percent. Additionally, inmate respondents at Riverbend Maximum Security Institution also reported the largest number of prior adult incarcerations (i.e., 4.05) throughout the state. Surveyed prisoners at Southeastern Tennessee State Regional Correctional Facility had the lowest mean number of 1.43 priors. On average, sampled inmates across Tennessee reported 2.18 prior incarcerations as an adult. However, subjects at both Northeast Correctional Complex and Turney Center Industrial Prison and Farm disclosed the highest mean rate of prior violence. About 46 percent of inmate subjects at each facility reported a prior incarceration for a violent offense. The least violent participants seemed to be housed at Southeastern Tennessee State Regional Correctional Facility. On average, 36 percent of sampled inmates in Tennessee had been incarcerated previously for a violent crime.

Prior gang involvement is the last importation variable explored in the present study. About 26 percent of inmate subjects at Northwest Correctional Complex had been involved in gang activities on the street during the year before their incarceration. However, only 3 percent of subjects at Northeast Correctional Complex admitted to previous gang involvement. On average, about 11 percent of sampled prisoners throughout Tennessee disclosed gang involvement while on the street.

In general, canvassed prisons in Tennessee appeared to have more imported sample characteristics than sampled institutions in Kentucky. In particular, Tennessee sampled prisons had a higher mean percentage of nonwhite inmates. On average, more subjects in Tennessee also disclosed prior incarcerations for a violent crime than did surveyed prisoners in Kentucky. Furthermore, participants in Tennessee reported more deprivations than did subjects in Kentucky.

Subjects in Tennessee scored slightly higher on the situational problems index than did respondents in Kentucky. The average score on this scale was 38 among inmate subjects in Tennessee. Interestingly, respondents at Riverbend Maximum Security Institution had the lowest mean score on this measure, while subjects in Turney Center Industrial Prison and Farm had the highest average score. Also, the average sentence length for surveyed inmates in Tennessee was 30.58 years. Inmate subjects at Northeast Correctional Complex reported the longest mean sentence length of 36.94 years, while respondents at Northwest Correctional Complex had the shortest average sentences of 23.03 years. Sampled inmates at Northeast had also served the most time at 10.50 years. Likewise, subjects at Northwest had served the least time with 6.20 years. On average, surveyed prisoners across Tennessee had served about 8.53 years of their current sentence.

Social relationships were again measured by visits and letters from family and friends, friendships formed inside prison, and associations with deviant inmates. In Tennessee, participants at Middle Tennessee Correctional Complex enjoyed the most visits from family and friends. Respondents at Northwest Correctional Complex received the most letters from family and friends. Subjects at South Central Correctional Facility reported the least amount of both visits and letters. In fact, inmate subjects at South Central reported the greatest degree of friendships formed inside prison throughout Tennessee. Sampled prisoners at Middle Tennessee formed the fewest inmate friendships. Furthermore, respondents at South Central disclosed that almost 2 of their friends inside prison were charged or could have been charged with misconduct during the past year. In contrast, subjects at Middle Tennessee Correctional Complex reported that only one of their close inside friends was deviant (i.e., charged or potentially charged with institutional misconduct). On average, sampled inmates throughout Tennessee revealed that they had somewhere between one and two deviant associates inside prison.

The final deprivation variable involved a measure of crowding from the inmates' perspective. According to inmate respondents, the most crowded institution in Tennessee was South Central Correctional Facility. The least crowded sampled prison in Tennessee appeared to be Middle Tennessee Correction Complex. On average, sampled prisoners in Tennessee reported that their institutions are somewhere between moderately and extremely crowded. Participants in Tennessee reported, on average, higher levels of crowding than did subjects in either Kentucky or Ohio. In addition, subjects throughout Tennessee disclosed prison conditions consistent with the deprivation perspective. In general, participants in Tennessee had longer sentences, had served more time, received fewer visits and letters from family and friends, had more prison friendships with more deviant associations, and experienced more crowding than respondents in either Kentucky or Ohio.

Across Tennessee, the control variables (i.e., self-esteem, definitions toward the rules, coping difficulties, and religious involvement) were not entirely revealing, with one exception. On average, 47 percent of sampled inmates reported some religious participation in the past year. Religious involvement within prison ranged from a low of 32 percent at South Central Correctional Facility to a high of 76 percent at Middle Tennessee Correctional Complex. Throughout the Tennessee sample, religious involvement in prison was slightly less than in Kentucky but about the same as in Ohio.

### Prisons in Ohio: Level 1

The characteristics of sampled prisons within Ohio varied just as they did within Kentucky and Tennessee. The mean level of prisonization for surveyed inmates in Ohio was the lowest among the three states. In particular, sampled prisoners in Pickaway Correctional Institution were the least prisonized, while subjects at Southern Ohio Correctional Facility scored highest on the prisonization scale among surveyed Ohioans. Likewise, respondents at Southern Ohio reported the greatest mean number (i.e., 3.71) of rule violations for the preceding year for any institution from Ohio, Tennessee, or Kentucky. Prisoners at Pickaway reported a mean number of .25 rule violations, the lowest in the state. However, on average, surveyed inmates in prisons throughout Ohio engaged in 1.90 acts of institutional misconduct.

The mean age in Ohio institutions was about the same as in Tennessee at 35.70. As previously mentioned, subjects at Dayton Correctional Institution were the youngest in the entire sample with a mean age of 23.80 years. The oldest group of participants was from Madison Correctional Institution where the average age was 43.75 years. Also at Madison, only about 8 percent of the inmate subjects were nonwhite. This was the lowest percentage of nonwhites across all three states. Ross Correctional Institution had the highest percentage of nonwhites with 80 percent for the entire sample. Additionally, sampled inmates in Ohio reported, on average, about 1.12 prior incarcerations. The mean number of previous incarcerations ranged from a low of .33 at Madison to a high of 1.84 at Warren Correctional Institution. Madison had the lowest reported priors for the entire sample. But at Ross, around 32 percent of inmate subjects had previously been incarcerated for a violent offense. Throughout Ohio, Southern Ohio Correctional Institution had the lowest percent (i.e., 14) of sampled inmates who had been incarcerated for a violent crime. On average, roughly 22 percent of participants in Ohio had previously been incarcerated for violence. Lastly, the mean rate of prior gang involvement disclosed by surveyed inmates in Ohio was 13 percent. Reported previous gang activities on the street ranged from a low of 4 percent at Chillicothe Correctional Institution to a high of 24 percent at Southeastern Correctional Institution.

Sample characteristics also involve the deprivations that exist throughout correctional institutions. Inmate subjects at Noble Correctional Institution perceived the most situational problems, while participants at Pickaway Correctional Institution disclosed the least amount of situational problems. The mean score (i.e., 37.99) on the situational problems index for Ohio was almost identical to that for Tennessee. The average sentence length in Ohio was less than 19 years with the mean length of time served falling around 7.6 years. Surveyed inmates at Dayton Correctional Complex had the shortest sentences, and subjects at Noble had the longest. However, respondents at London Correctional Institution had served an average of 11.17 years, the longest in the entire sample. Subjects at Pickaway had served only 3.26 years, the shortest across the three state sub-samples.

In terms of social contacts, subjects at Warren Correctional Institution received, on average, the greatest mean amount of visits from family and friends. Surveyed prisoners at Madison Correctional Institution received the most letters from family and friends. Sampled convicts at Ross Correctional Institution received the least visits, whereas respondents at Pickaway got the least amount of letters. Throughout Ohio, respondents at Southern Ohio Correctional Institution formed the most friendships, while participants at Warren Correctional formed the least. On average, sampled inmates in Ohio reported associating with very few deviant peers. In fact, the mean number of close friends inside prison who had been charged or could have been charged for institutional misconduct was .90. Inmate subjects at Madison Correctional reported the greatest average number of deviant friends, whereas prisoners in Chillicothe had the lowest mean number (i.e., .44) of deviant peers across the entire sample.

Crowding in the Ohio sample was greater than in Kentucky but less than in Tennessee. On average, surveyed inmates in Ohio indicated that their institutions were moderately crowded. Dayton Correctional Institution appeared the least crowded while Chillicothe was the most crowded. Lastly, most of the control variables did not yield interesting results. The mean rate of religious participation was 46 percent across the Ohio subsample. About 28 percent of inmate subjects at Chillicothe reported involvement in religious services during the past year. In contrast, Orient Correctional Institution had the highest rate of religious participation within Ohio at 58 percent.

**Level 1 Variables Between Three States**

The mean values for Level 1 variables appear unequal across Kentucky, Tennessee, and Ohio. In fact, several notable findings emerge upon closer inspection. The mean levels of 11 Level 1 variables were higher in Tennessee than in Kentucky or Ohio. In particular, inmate subjects in Tennessee seemed to be more prisonized, older, and more violent. On average, sampled Tennesseans also reported more situational problems, longer sentences, more time served, more friendships inside prison, more deviant associations inside prison, and greater coping difficulties than respondents in either Kentucky or Ohio. Additionally, surveyed inmates in Tennessee reported lower mean numbers of visits and letters from family and friends, and less self-esteem than subjects in the other two states. Thus, it appears as if the context of imprisonment in the Tennessee sample is markedly different from that in Kentucky or Ohio.

Analysis of variance (ANOVA) was again used to determine the significance of the apparent differences in the mean values of continuous, Level 1 variables between the three states. Specifically, significant F ratios were obtained on the following Level 1 variables: rule violations, prior incarcerations, sentence length, time served, visits from family and friends, letters from family and friends, deviant associations, and crowding. That is, the mean values for each of these variables were not equal across the Kentucky, Tennessee, and Ohio sub-samples. However, the mean levels of prisonization, age, situational problems, prison friendships, self-esteem, definitions, and coping difficulties were equal between the three states samples.

Bonferroni multiple comparisons tests confirmed that inmate subjects in Tennessee felt, on average, more crowded than respondents in Ohio or Kentucky. Sampled Tennesseans also reported a significantly higher mean number of deviant associations than did respondents in Ohio. Participants in Tennessee received significantly fewer visits and letters than inmate subjects in Kentucky. Furthermore, on average, surveyed convicts in Tennessee were serving longer sentences than respondents in Kentucky or Ohio. Lastly, the mean amount of time served was longer for subjects in prisons throughout Tennessee than surveyed prisoners in Ohio or Kentucky. However, on average, sampled convicts in Kentucky had more prior incarcerations than participants in Tennessee or Ohio. The mean number of rule violations was significantly higher in Ohio than in Kentucky. On average, sampled inmates in Tennessee reported more rule violations than did respondents in Kentucky.

## Level 1 Variables Between Thirty Prisons

Analysis of variance (ANOVA) was also used to determine if the means of Level 1 variables were equal between the thirty sampled correctional institutions. The following continuous variables had F statistics at the .01 significance level: prisonization (i.e., $F=2.64$), rule violations (i.e.,

F=3.45), prior incarcerations (i.e., F=2.99), sentence length (i.e, F=4.26), time served (i.e., F=5.23), outside visits (i.e., F=4.45), outside letters (i.e., F=4.68), crowding (i.e., 8.25), and individual definitions toward the rules (i.e., F=1.81). In particular, the two dependent variables had unequal means across the thirty prisons. With a significant F ratio of 2.64, the mean levels of prisonization were not equal between the thirty penitentiaries. Likewise, the significant F statistic obtained for rule violations indicates that the means on this variable were also unequal between the thirty prisons.

Post hoc tests revealed that the mean level of prisonization was significantly higher at South Central Correctional Facility in Ohio than Middle Tennessee Correctional Complex or Pickaway Correctional Institution. The mean level of prisonization was also greater at Northeast Correctional Complex than either Middle Tennessee or Pickaway. Additionally, the average degree of prisonization was higher at Northwest Correctional Complex than Middle Tennessee. Lastly, the average level of prisonization was greater at South Central Correctional Complex than Middle Tennessee Correctional Complex as well. It is interesting to note that most of the sampled facilities with higher mean levels of prisonization were located in Tennessee.

Bonferonni multiple comparisons also shed light on the significant differences in the mean number of rule violations between the thirty prisons. Northwest Correctional Complex and Southern Ohio Correctional Facility stood out as having exceptionally high average numbers of rule infractions. Specifically, the average number of rule violations at Northwest was larger than the mean number at Blackburn Correctional Complex, Frankfort Career Development Center, Green River Correctional Complex, Western Kentucky Correctional Complex, Middle Tennessee Correctional Complex and Morgan County Correctional Complex. The mean number of rule infractions at Southern Ohio was also higher than the average number of tickets given at Blackburn, Frankfort, Green River, Western Kentucky, Middle Tennessee, or Morgan County.

In sum, the ANOVAs illustrate that groups of sampled prisoners were substantially differentiated on a variety of factors. These tests indicated that there was significant heterogeneity between different correctional contexts. However, it is possible that the results of the ANOVAs were influenced by the sampling procedures used in each state. Analysis of variance works best with groups that have been randomly sampled from normal populations. Given the problems with attaining random samples in the present study, the results from the ANOVA procedures may be questionable. Particularly in Ohio, systematic random sampling techniques were sacrificed in order to obtain access to their facilities.

## Official Versus Self-report Data

A comparison of self-report data with official information should illustrate any bias that may have been introduced during sampling. Unfortunately, only demographic information is typically available from official sources. As such, only sample statistics with official statistics for age and race were comparable. Table 5.5 shows the sample statistics and official statistics on both age (i.e., percent under 25) and race (i.e., percent nonwhite) for each correctional facility included in this project.

In regard to age, the most striking differences between sample and official data were found in Tennessee and Ohio. For example, about 55 percent of surveyed inmates at Northwest Correctional Complex in Tennessee were under 25 years old. However, official counts indicated that about 23 percent of inmates at this facility were under 25 years. At Dayton Correctional Institution, roughly 70 percent of surveyed prisoners were under 25, while official data revealed that only 51 percent of that population was under 25 years. Furthermore, greater percentages of young inmates in twelve of the thirty prisons were obtained in the sample.

For race, the most extreme differences between self-report and official data occurred in Ohio. About 80 percent of the inmates surveyed at Ross Correctional Institution were nonwhite. Official sources suggested that the population is only 52 percent nonwhite. Likewise, at Pickaway Correctional Institution, about 63 percent nonwhite subjects were surveyed while the nonwhite population was only 51 percent according to official sources. Nonwhite inmates were also over-sampled in Tennessee. At Riverbend Maximum Security Institution, about 65 percent of surveyed inmates were nonwhite. Official sources indicate that Riverbend's population is only 52 percent nonwhite. Lastly, according to official data, about 54 percent of the inmate population at Turney Center Industrial Prison and Farm were nonwhite, whereas about 73 percent nonwhite inmates were sampled there.

Table 5.5
Sample Statistics Versus Official Statistics ($n_j$=30)

|         | Percent Under 25 | | Percent Nonwhite | |
|---------|--------|----------|--------|----------|
| Prison  | Sample | Official | Sample | Official |
| *KY*    |        |          |        |          |
| BCFC    | 21     | 26       | 39     | 27       |
| BCC     | 16     | 11       | 47     | 36       |
| EKCC    | 15     | 25       | 37     | 35       |
| FCDC    | 5      | 9        | 36     | 47       |
| GRCC    | 18     | 19       | 38     | 34       |
| KSP     | 25     | 21       | 45     | 30       |
| KSR     | 15     | 12       | 12     | 8        |
| LLCC    | 5      | 15       | 37     | 35       |
| NTC     | 31     | 26       | 42     | 47       |
| RCC     | 15     | 6        | 52     | 31       |
| WKCC    | 10     | 15       | 29     | 32       |
| *TN*    |        |          |        |          |
| MTCC    | 10     | 15       | 57     | 58       |
| MCCC    | 6      | 10       | 21     | 27       |
| RMSI    | 10     | 9        | 65     | 52       |
| NECC    | 9      | 7        | 21     | 27       |
| NWCC    | 55     | 23       | 74     | 65       |
| SCCF    | 14     | 10       | 49     | 53       |
| STSRCF  | 3      | 6        | 34     | 41       |
| TCIPF   | 12     | 10       | 73     | 54       |
| *OH*    |        |          |        |          |
| CCI     | 4      | 10       | 41     | 40       |
| DCI     | 70     | 51       | 70     | 67       |
| LCI     | 13     | 28       | 33     | 49       |
| MCI     | 8      | 19       | 8      | 40       |
| NCI     | 25     | 37       | 23     | 41       |
| OCI     | 8      | 11       | 50     | 55       |
| PCI     | 6      | 19       | 63     | 51       |
| RCI     | 22     | 22       | 80     | 52       |
| SCI     | 31     | 44       | 38     | 52       |
| SOCF    | 17     | 16       | 68     | 62       |
| WCI     | 14     | 21       | 41     | 48       |

In spite of these discrepancies, the overall sample appears to be fairly representative of the populations throughout the thirty correctional facilities. For instance, according to official sources, about 17.2 percent of the inmate population for these thirty state institutions was under age 25. This official statistic was derived by summing the state's count of inmates under age 25 across the 30 institutions and then dividing by the total population of the 30 facilities in this study. In regard to the survey data, about 17.4 of the sample was under age 25. For race, about 44.2 percent of the inmate population for the sampled prisons was nonwhite according to official sources. Again, this official statistic was derived by summing the number of nonwhite inmates across the 30 institutions and then dividing by the total population of the 30 facilities in the project. About 43.5 percent of the surveyed sample was nonwhite. The similarities between self-report and official data for these two variables are quite remarkable.

## Correctional Contexts

The context of corrections varies from prison to prison and state to state. The historical similarities between corrections in Kentucky, Tennessee, and Ohio have been replaced by divergent modern themes. The experience of imprisonment at facilities such as Blackburn Correctional Complex, Frankfort Career Development Center, and Middle Tennessee Correctional Complex is markedly different from that at Kentucky State Penitentiary, Northwest Correctional Complex, Northeast Correctional Complex, and Southern Ohio Correctional Facility. The preliminary analyses conducted in this chapter establish that differences in correctional context between prisons and between states certainly exist.

# CHAPTER 6

# A Multilevel Analysis of Prisonization

This multilevel analysis of prisonization consists of two phases. The first stage involves an exploration of the direct effects on prisonization of both Level 1 and Level 2 antecedents (i.e., deprivation and importation variables) and the conditioning influences that Level 2 factors have upon Level 1 effects. The second phase entails an examination of the direct effects on misconduct of both micro and macro predictors, including prisonization, and the moderating influences of macro variables on micro effects. In the present chapter, the results of hierarchical linear regression models are revealed. The first part of the chapter involves a discussion of the antecedents of prisonization, and the second section explores misconduct as a primary consequence of prisonization. For both sections, a null model, a random-coefficients model, and a contextual model are tested. However, a few words about the associations between the micro and macro variables are in order before discussing the multilevel analyses.

## Associations Between Variables

Bivariate correlations revealed the associations between research variables. Prisonization and institutional misconduct were correlated in the expected direction. A high degree of prisonization appeared to be associated with many rule violations. However, expectations concerning the correlations between prisonization and the independent variables were only partially confirmed. At the micro level, a high degree of prisonization was positively correlated with a number of antecedents, including prior gang involvement, situational problems, the number of deviant prison associates, the perception of crowding, and coping difficulties. These correlation coefficients ranged from a low of .075 to a high of .226. Furthermore, high prisonization was also negatively correlated with several micro predictors, such as age, race, sentence length, time served, individual definitions toward the rules, and religious participation inside prison. Contrary to deprivation theory, longer

*127*

sentences were inversely related to higher prisonization. Correlation coefficients for these variables went from -.064 to -.231. Surprisingly, a higher degree of prisonization was not associated with the number of prior incarcerations, prior violence, the amount of visits and letters from family and friends, or self-esteem.

Prisonization was also correlated with a few macro variables. In particular, a higher level of prisonization was positively associated with institutional factors like security level, gang presence, and the percentage of nonwhite inmates. These correlation coefficients ranged from a low of .065 to a high of .138. Prisonization appeared unrelated to several prison-level variables such as the prison's age, the number of educational and vocational programs, crowding, the percent under 25 years old, the inmate population, and the inmate-to-staff ratio.

Institutional misconduct was measured as the number of tickets or rule violations issued to the respondents in the past year. Five micro and five macro variables were correlated with this dependent variable. Only prior gang involvement and a perception of crowding were positively associated with larger numbers of rule violations. Also at the micro level, greater misconduct was negatively correlated with age, the number of visits from family and friends, and associations with deviant prison friends. The correlation coefficients for these micro variables ranged from .068 to .198. At the macro level, a greater number of rule violations was positively correlated with the number of educational and vocational programs, gang presence, percent nonwhite, and the inmate population. Negative correlations were observed for only the age of the institution. Coefficients went from .076 to .157. These findings suggest that the integrated deprivation-importation model may not be the best explanation for misconduct inside prison.

Furthermore, it is important to note that higher numbers of prison programs were associated with more acts of institutional misconduct. Although this finding contradicts deprivation theory, there are other reasons to expect such a finding. For instance, it may be that programs provide opportunities for offenders to engage in more misconduct. However, it may be that prison programs teach lower-class skills to inmates yet instill middle-class values. The ensuing strain and frustration generated by this disjuncture of goals and means may, in turn, lead to increased rule violations.

The bivariate correlations also reveal additional important points about the associations between variables. First, Level 1 variables can approximate Level 2 factors in multilevel analyses. However, no correlation coefficients above .22 were discovered between micro and macro variables. This suggests that no Level 1 variables were estimating Level 2 factors.

Second, highly correlated variables may indicate multicollinearity. However, the significant bivariate correlations between the micro, independent variables indicated only low to moderate associations. The largest correlation coefficient (i.e., .578) was discovered between sentence length and time served. It certainly stands to reason that inmates with longer sentences would have, on average, served more time than inmates with shorter sentences. Furthermore, a large correlation coefficient of .568 was found for situational problems and coping difficulties. It stands to reason that these two measures would be somewhat related. That is, one would expect an individual to report more situational problems if he experiences a lot of coping difficulties inside prison. The Level 2 variables were also moderately correlated with one exception. The correlation coefficient between the number of programs and the inmate population was .747. However, it is reasonable to believe that prisons with greater populations must offer more educational and vocational programs than prisons with smaller populations. Nonetheless, these variables should be used with caution in the multivariate analysis.

## The Antecedents of Prisonization

### The Null Model

In order to use hierarchical linear modeling (HLM), significant variation in the mean level of prisonization across institutional contexts must first be demonstrated. It is appropriate to use HLM only if the dependent variable (i.e., scores on the prisonization index) varies across different contexts. Table 6.1 shows the null model for prisonization. In the null model, only the dependent variable is allowed to vary across contexts. The null model demonstrates variation across the micro and macro units of analysis. This variation across contexts is referred to as an intraclass

Table 6.1
Null Model for Prisonization:
Variance at the Inmate and Prison Levels[a]

| Random Effects | Variance Component | z-Score |
|---|---|---|
| Level 2 Variance Mean Prisonization Score | 4.927[b] | 2.32 |
| Level 1 Variance | 105.894 | 22.64 |

[a]$N$=1,054 inmates (Level 1); $N$=30 prisons (Level 2)
[b]Intraclass Correlation [(4.927/110.821)*100]=4.445

correlation. The intraclass correlation is computed by dividing the variance at Level 2 (i.e., 4.927) by the sum of the variance at Levels 1 and 2 (i.e., 110.821) then multiplying by 100. Thus, an intraclass correlation of 4.5 for prisonization indicates that 4.5 percent of the variation in the mean level of prisonization occurs at the institutional level. The majority of the variation (i.e., 95.5 percent) in the mean level of prisonization is at the individual level. Although this intraclass correlation is low, it is still significant and suggests that context is important in fully understanding prisonization.

The Random Coefficients Model
After a significant intraclass correlation has been obtained for the dependent variable, the next step of hierarchical linear modeling involves estimating a random coefficients model. Specifically, the effects on prisonization of the Level 1 antecedents are allowed to vary across penitentiaries. The Level 1 equation with prisonization as the dependent variable is represented as follows:

$(Prisonization)_{ij} = \beta_{0j} + \beta_{1j}(age)_{ij} + \beta_{2j}(race)_{ij} + \beta_{3j}(prior\ incarcerations)_{ij} + \beta_{4j}(prior\ violent\ offenses)_{ij} + \beta_{5j}(prior\ gang\ involvement)_{ij} + \beta_{6j}(situational\ problems)_{ij} + \beta_{7j}(sentence\ length)_{ij} + \beta_{8j}(time\ served)_{ij} + \beta_{9j}(visits)_{ij} +$

$\beta_{10j}$(letters)$_{ij}$ + $\beta_{11j}$(friends inside prison)$_{ij}$ + $\beta_{12j}$(deviant prison associates)$_{ij}$ + $\beta_{13j}$(crowding perception)$_{ij}$ + $\beta_{14j}$(self-esteem)$_{ij}$ + $\beta_{15j}$(general definitions toward the law)$_{ij}$ + $\beta_{16j}$(coping difficulties)$_{ij}$ + $\beta_{17j}$(religious involvement)$_{ij}$ + $e_{ij}$                                               (6.1)

Since all slopes are allowed to vary in the random coefficients model, the Level 2 equation was specified in the following manner:

$$\beta_{kj} = \Theta_{k0} + U_{kj} \text{ for k=0 through 17} \qquad (6.2)$$

The statistical test of this model with MLwiN software indicated that not every Level 1 antecedent varied in its effect on prisonization across institutions. Table 6.2 illustrates the reduced random coefficients regression model. Note that the mean score of prisonization no longer significantly varies across prisons. It approaches significance at the .10 level. This finding was unexpected since micro antecedents should not account for variation in the dependent event across prisons. Wilcox Rountree and Clayton (1999) also encountered this problem in their multilevel examination of adolescent alcohol use. When their random coefficients model was specified, the intercept became non-significant. There are several reasons for this phenomenon. The most plausible one is that Level 1 factors are approximating Level 2 variables in the model.

However, the intercept (i.e., the mean score of prisonization) was treated as random because its original variance component across prisons was significant. Using the formula, [1-(1.760/4.927)*100], there was a 64 percent reduction in the value of the Level 2 variance component for the intercept when comparing the null model with the random coefficients model. Micro antecedents appear to account for a sizable proportion of the cross-level variation in prisonization.

Only one micro antecedent (i.e., general definitions about the rules) varied across prison contexts. The Level 1 variables in Table 6.2 were then fixed, and the Level 2 equation (i.e., 6.2) was amended as follows:

$$\beta_{0j} = \Theta_{00} + U_{0j} \qquad (6.3)$$
$$\beta_{15j} = \Theta_{150} + U_{15j} \qquad (6.4)$$
$$\beta_{kj} = \Theta_{k0} \text{ for k=1 through 14 and 16 through 17} \qquad (6.5)$$

Table 6.2
The Reduced Random Coefficients Model for Prisonization

| Fixed Effects | Coefficient | Standard Error | t-Ratio |
|---|---|---|---|
| Constant (mean prisonization) | 40.544 | .386 | 105.04 |
| Age of Inmate | -.188 | .031 | -6.06 |
| Race | -1.477 | .613 | -2.41 |
| Prior Gang Involvement | 2.956 | .918 | 3.22 |
| Situational Problems | .175 | .031 | 5.65 |
| Perception of Crowding | 1.081 | .294 | 3.68 |
| General Definitions | -.518 | .124 | -4.18 |
| Religious Involvement | -3.172 | .595 | -5.33 |

| Random Effects | Variance Component | z-Score | p-value |
|---|---|---|---|
| Mean Prisonization Score | 1.760 | 1.58 | >.10 |
| General Definitions (about the rules) | .238 | 2.07 | <.10 |
| Level 1 Variance | 84.539 | 22.35 | <.10 |

Equation 6.4 indicates that the effect on prisonization of an inmate's general definitions toward the rules varied across correctional facilities. The "average" main effect of this variable suggests that general, prosocial attitudes toward the rules are predictive of lower levels of prisonization. However, the significant variance component suggests that this "average" effect differs substantially, depending upon the prison context in question. The effects of all other micro antecedents were constant across sampled prisons.

Several micro antecedents had significant main, fixed effects on prisonization. From importation theory, age, race, and prior gang involvement significantly influenced the degree of prisonization. Specifically, age and prisonization were inversely related, indicating that older subjects were less prisonized. Also, the mean score of prisonization was almost 1.5 points lower for nonwhites than whites. Prior gang involvement had a large impact on prisonization. In particular, subjects who reported gang involvement on the street had a mean prisonization score 2.956 points higher than respondents who did not reveal any prior gang activities. Both previous incarcerations and prior violence had no significant effects on prisonization. Furthermore, only two variables from the deprivation perspective significantly affected prisonization. As expected, situational problems were positively associated with prisonization. Also, more acute perceptions of crowding were predictive of high prisonization. Surprisingly, this analysis failed to reveal an effect on prisonization for sentence length, time served, or the quadratic expression of time served. In sum, it appears as if both importation and deprivation variables are important in understanding prisonization at Level 1.

In addition to the theoretically derived antecedents, two of the control variables had significant effects on prisonization. As already mentioned, respondents who had more general prosocial definitions towards the rules were less prisonized. Also, subjects who were involved in religious activities reported less prisonization. Interestingly, the mean prisonization score for subjects who reported religious involvement in prison within the past year was 3.17 points lower than respondents who had not been involved in religious activities.

## The Contextual Model

The final step of hierarchical linear modeling involves the full contextual model when Level 2 variables are included in order to account for both the variation in the mean prisonization score and the variation in the effect of general definitions. Table 6.3 presents the results once the contextual variables are included in the model.

Table 6.3
The Reduced Contextual Model for Prisonization

| Fixed Effects | Coefficient | Standard Error | t-Ratio |
|---|---|---|---|
| Constant (mean prisonization) | 40.573 | .290 | 139.91 |
| Age of Prison | -.029 | .014 | -2.07 |
| Security Level | 3.471 | .992 | 3.50 |
| Percent Under 25 years old | -6.513 | 3.595 | -1.81 |
| Age of Inmate | -.200 | .031 | -6.45 |
| Race | -1.533 | .601 | -2.55 |
| Prior Gang Involvement | 2.960 | .916 | 4.93 |
| Situational Problems | .172 | .030 | 5.73 |
| Perception of Crowding | 1.057 | .283 | 3.73 |
| General Definitions | -.515 | .127 | -4.06 |
| Religious Involvement | -3.165 | .590 | -5.39 |

| Random Effect | Variance Component | z-Score | p-value |
|---|---|---|---|
| Mean Prisonization Score | .000 | .00 | >.05 |
| General Definitions (about the rules) | .256 | 2.15 | <.05 |
| Level 1 Variance | 84.425 | 22.65 | <.05 |

The following two Level 2 equations were initially tested during this phase:

$\beta_{0j} = \Theta_{00} + \Theta_{01}(\text{Prison Age}) + \Theta_{02}(\text{Security Level}) + \Theta_{03}(\text{Number of Programs}) + \Theta_{04}(\text{Crowding}) + \Theta_{05}(\text{Gangs}) + \Theta_{06}(\text{Percent Nonwhite}) + \Theta_{07}(\text{Percent Under 25}) + \Theta_{08}(\text{Population}) + \Theta_{09}(\text{Inmate/staff Ratio}) + \Theta_{10}(\text{Kentucky}) + \Theta_{11}(\text{Tennessee}) + U_{0j}$     (6.6)
*and*

$\beta_{15j} = \Theta_{150} + \Theta_{151}$(Prison Age) + $\Theta_{152}$(Security Level) + $\Theta_{153}$(Number of Programs) + $\Theta_{154}$(Crowding) + $\Theta_{155}$(Gangs) + $\Theta_{156}$(Percent Nonwhite) + $\Theta_{157}$(Percent Under 25) + $\Theta_{158}$(Population) + $\Theta_{159}$(Inmate/staff Ratio) + $\Theta_{1510}$(Kentucky) + $\Theta_{1511}$(Tennessee) + $U_{15j}$ (6.7)

when $\beta_{kj} = \Theta_{k0}$ for k=1 through 14 and 16 through 17 (6.8)

In order to stabilize the contextual model, Level 2 variables were added and dropped in a step-wise fashion. Hierarchical linear modeling revealed that only the age of the prison, the security level designation, and the percentage of the population under 25 years old significantly affected the variance in prisonization across correctional facilities. As such, equation 6.6 was "reduced" and re-specified as follows:

$\beta_{0j} = \Theta_{00} + \Theta_{01}$(Prison Age) + $\Theta_{02}$(Security Level) + $\Theta_{07}$(Percent Under 25 years old) (6.9)

There was a total reduction in the variation in the score of prisonization across correctional facilities once these Level 2 variables were included in the model. In fact, once Level 2 predictors are included in the model, the Level 2 variation in prisonization disappeared.

HLM also indicated that none of the Level 2 factors significantly explained the variance in the effect of general prosocial definitions on prisonization across correctional institutions. Equation 6.7 was amended:

$\beta_{15j} = \Theta_{150} + U_{15j}$ (6.10)

Although no significant Level 2 factors could account for the variance in this effect across prisons, its variance component was reduced. In other words, the variance component for the slope coefficient of general definitions also declined when Level 2 variables were included in the model. Using the formula, $[(1-.177/.238)*100]$, the variation in the effect of general definitions on prisonization was reduced by about 25 percent.

Several structural Level 2 antecedents had significant main, fixed effects on prisonization. In particular, as the age of the prison decreased, so too did prisonization. This is contrary to what one would expect from deprivation theory. One would suspect that older facilities would present harsher living conditions, which would result in heightened feelings of deprivation. Incidentally, the average prisonization score for subjects in maximum security prisons was 3.47 points higher than the mean for respondents in non-maximum security institutions. This finding is quite consistent with deprivation theory and the work of Sykes (1958), and it suggests that harsher living conditions in maximum security correctional facilities causes prisonization.

A few elements of prison culture also affected prisonization directly. As the percentage of inmates under 25 years old increased, prisonization declined. Again, this is a rather counterintuitive finding. Thus, it appears as if prisonization is higher in newer, maximum security correctional facilities with populations that are comprised of a lower percentage of inmates under 25 years old. However, none of the state dummy variables were significant in this model. In short, the features of correctional facilities influence individual social phenomena (i.e., prisonization) on the inside. Consequently, in spite of the contextual variables that were introduced into the model, the micro antecedents of prisonization still remained significant.

In order to explain the variation in the effect on prisonization of general, prosocial definitions, several cross-level interactions were examined. Unfortunately, none of these interactions could adequately account for the variation in the slope of general definitions. In fact, when the interaction terms were entered into the model in a step-wise fashion, none approached significance. It is likely that some other unmeasured feature of correctional institutions may be influencing the variance in the effect of general prosocial definitions on prisonization across correctional communities.

## A Consequence of Prisonization: Misconduct

### The Null Model

As with prisonization, a multilevel exploration of misconduct as a consequence of socialization inside prison entails a number of steps. Table 6.4 reveals the null model for rule violations. As noted previously,

Table 6.4
Null Model for Rule Violations[a]:
Variance at the Inmate and Prison Levels[b]

| Random Effects | Variance Component | z-Score |
|---|---|---|
| Level 2 Variance<br>Mean Rule Violations | .062[c] | 3.10 |
| Level 1 Variance | .476 | 22.66 |

[a]The natural logarithm of rule violations
[b]$N=1,054$ inmates (Level 1); $N=30$ prisons (Level 2)
[c]Intraclass Correlation [(.062/.538)*100]=11.52

the frequency distribution of rule violations was somewhat skewed. As such, it was smoothed by a logarithmic transformation that involved adding a constant (i.e., 1) to all scores and then taking the natural log of this sum. The purpose of the null model is to determine if there is significant variation in the mean level of the dependent variable (i.e., rule violations in this case) to merit hierarchical linear modeling (HLM). There is significant variation in rule violations across prisons. The intraclass correlation of 11.5 percent was obtained by dividing the Level 2 variance by the total variance at both levels of analysis and multiplying by 100. As with prisonization, the majority of the variation (i.e., 88.50 percent) in the mean level of rule violations occurs at the micro level. However, the variation in rule violations across correctional facilities is still significant. Thus, it is feasible to proceed with hierarchical linear modeling.

The Random Coefficients Model
The random coefficients model is essentially a test to determine which effects on rule violations of independent Level 1 factors vary across prisons. The Level 1 equation for rule violations as the dependent variable is specified in the following manner:

(Rule violations)$_{ij}$ = $\beta_{0j}$ + $\beta_{1j}$(age)$_{ij}$ + $\beta_{2j}$(race)$_{ij}$ + $\beta_{3j}$(prior incarcerations)$_{ij}$ + $\beta_{4j}$(prior violent offenses)$_{ij}$ + $\beta_{5j}$(prior gang involvement)$_{ij}$ + $\beta_{6j}$(situational problems)$_{ij}$ + $\beta_{7j}$(sentence length)$_{ij}$ + $\beta_{8j}$(time served)$_{ij}$ + $\beta_{9j}$(visits)$_{ij}$ + $\beta_{10j}$(letters)$_{ij}$ + $\beta_{11j}$(friends inside prison)$_{ij}$ + $\beta_{12j}$(deviant prison associates)$_{ij}$ + $\beta_{13j}$(crowding perception)$_{ij}$ + $\beta_{14j}$(self-esteem)$_{ij}$ + $\beta_{15j}$(general definitions toward the rules)$_{ij}$ + $\beta_{16j}$(coping difficulties)$_{ij}$ + $\beta_{17j}$(religious involvement)$_{ij}$ + $\beta_{18j}$(prisonization)$_{ij}$ + $e_{ij}$ $\qquad$ (6.11)

Again, since all slopes are initially allowed to vary in the random coefficients model, the Level 2 equation was represented as follows:

$$\beta_{kj} = \Theta_{k0} + U_{kj} \text{ for k=0 through 18} \qquad (6.12)$$

However, the statistical test of this model with MLwiN software revealed that no Level 1 parameters varied across prisons.

Table 6.5 displays the random coefficients model for rule violations without prisonization as a predictor variable. The constant still significantly varied across correctional facilities once the micro predictors were included in the model, but its contextual variance declined. Using the formula, [1-(.040/.062)*100], there was about a 35 percent reduction in the value of the Level 2 variance component for the intercept when comparing the null model with the random coefficients model. As with prisonization, Level 1 predictors appear to account for some of the cross-level variation in rule violations as a dependent variable.

Since no micro predictors varied in their effects on rule violations, the non-varying Level 1 factors were fixed, and the Level 2 equations were revised as follows:

$$\beta_{0j} = \Theta_{00} + U_{0j} \qquad (6.13)$$
$$\beta_{kj} = \Theta_{k0} \text{ for k=1 through 18} \qquad (6.14)$$

Four Level 1 variables had significant main, fixed effects on institutional misconduct. First, from importation theory, the age of the inmate and prior gang involvement affected the natural logarithm of rule violations inside prison. Specifically, as the age of the inmate increased, rule violations declined. Also, the mean level of rule violations for those

Table 6.5
The Reduced Random Coefficients Model for Rule Violations[a]

| Fixed Effects | Coefficient | Standard Error | t-Ratio |
|---|---|---|---|
| Constant (mean rule violations) | .570 | .043 | 13.26 |
| Age of Inmate | -.012 | .002 | -6.00 |
| Prior Gang Involvement | .315 | .066 | 4.77 |
| Visits from family and friends | -.026 | .013 | -2.00 |
| Prison friendships | -.055 | .022 | -2.50 |
| Deviant prison associates | .040 | .012 | 3.33 |
| Perception of Crowding | .062 | .022 | 2.82 |

| Random Effects | Variance Component | z-Score | p-value |
|---|---|---|---|
| Mean Rule Violations | .040 | 2.86 | <.05 |
| Level 1 Variance | .442 | 22.10 | <.05 |

[a]Model without prisonization as a predictor variable.

inmate subjects who reported gang involvement in the year prior to their incarceration was higher than those respondents who disclosed no prior gang activities on the street. From the deprivation perspective, the number of visits from family and friends had an inverse relationship with misconduct. In particular, as visits from family and friends increased, the number of rule violations decreased. Another deprivation variable, the perception of crowding, also had a significant effect on institutional misconduct. As an inmate's perception of crowding increased, so too did his number of rule violations. Also, as expected, when associations with deviant inmate friends increased inside prison, so too did the subject's number of rule violations. Surprisingly, neither sentence length, time

served, nor the quadratic expression of time served had a significant effect
on misconduct. Likewise, contrary to the deprivation perspective, as the
number of prison friendships increased inside prison, inmates reported less
institutional misconduct. In sum, two importation variables and four
deprivation variables at Level 1 influenced the extent of misconduct inside
prison. It appears as if the deprivation model may be more useful than
importation theory at explaining rule violations among prisoners.

Lastly, prisonization (i.e., a normative orientation caused by both
importation and deprivation variables) was significantly associated with
institutional misconduct. Table 6.6 illustrates the random coefficients
model for rule violations when prisonization is included. Specifically, as
a subject's degree of prisonization increased, so too did his extent of rule
violations inside prison. By including prisonization in the model, the
effects of other Level 1 predictor variables were diminished, and the effect
on misconduct of visits from family and friends became non-significant.
In this sense, prisonization mediated the effects of Level 1 importation and
deprivation variables. The Level 2 variance component for mean rule
violations also decreased, but its significance was not affected.

### The Contextual Model

The purpose of the full contextual model is to determine which Level 2
variables are useful in explaining Level 2 variation in the mean number of
rule violations. Table 6.7 presents the results once the macro variables are
incorporated into the model. The following Level 2 equation was tested:

$\beta_{0j} = \Theta_{00} + \Theta_{01}(\text{Prison Age}) + \Theta_{02}(\text{Security Level}) + \Theta_{03}(\text{Number of Programs}) + \Theta_{04}(\text{Crowding}) + \Theta_{05}(\text{Gangs}) + \Theta_{06}(\text{Percent Nonwhite}) + \Theta_{07}(\text{Percent Under 25}) + \Theta_{08}(\text{Population}) + \Theta_{09}(\text{Inmate/staff Ratio}) + \Theta_{10}(\text{Kentucky}) + \Theta_{11}(\text{Tennessee}) + U_{0j}$ $\qquad$ (6.15)

*and*

$\beta_{kj} = \Theta_{k0}$ for k=1 through 18 $\qquad\qquad$ (6.16)

Table 6.6
A Reduced Random Coefficients Model:
The Effect of Prisonization on Rule Violations[a]

| Fixed Effects | Coefficient | Standard Error | t-Ratio |
|---|---|---|---|
| Constant (mean rule violations) | .571 | .041 | 13.93 |
| Age of Inmate | -.011 | .002 | -5.50 |
| Prior Gang Involvement | .301 | .067 | 4.49 |
| Visits from family and friends | -.024 | .013 | -1.85 |
| Prison friendships | -.055 | .021 | -2.61 |
| Deviant prison associates | .039 | .012 | 3.25 |
| Perception of Crowding | .056 | .022 | 2.54 |
| Prisonization | .005 | .002 | 3.00 |

| Random Effects | Variance Component | z-Score | p-value |
|---|---|---|---|
| Mean Rule Violations | .037 | 2.85 | <.05 |
| Level 1 Variance | .441 | 23.21 | <.05 |

[a]Model with prisonization as a predictor of logged rule violations.

As indicated by Table 6.7, the variation of the mean number of rule violations across prisons was reduced by 49 percent (i.e., [1-(.019/.037)*100]) from the random coefficients model once the Level 2 variables were added. Two macro predictors had significant main effects on misconduct. Equation 6.15 was reduced as follows:

$$\beta_{0j} = \Theta_{00} + \Theta_{05}(\text{Gang Presence}) + \Theta_{10}(\text{Kentucky}) + \Theta_{11}(\text{Tennessee}) + U_{0j} \tag{6.17}$$

*and*

$$\beta_{kj} = \Theta_{k0} \text{ for k=1 through 18} \tag{6.18}$$

Table 6.7
The Reduced Contextual Model for Rule Violations

| Fixed Effects | Coefficient | Standard Error | t-Ratio |
|---|---|---|---|
| Constant (mean rule violations) | .575 | .034 | 16.91 |
| Gang Presence | 1.921 | .752 | 2.55 |
| Kentucky | -.182 | .070 | -2.60 |
| Age of Inmate | -.011 | .002 | -5.50 |
| Prior Gang Involvement | .295 | .067 | 4.40 |
| Visits from family and friends | -.023 | .013 | -1.77 |
| Prison friendships | -.058 | .021 | -2.76 |
| Deviant prison associates | .039 | .012 | 3.25 |
| Perception of Crowding | .049 | .022 | 2.23 |
| Prisonization | .005 | .002 | 2.50 |

| Random Effect | Variance Component | z-Score | p-value |
|---|---|---|---|
| Mean Rule Violations | .019 | 2.11 | <.05 |
| Level 1 Variance | .441 | 23.21 | <.05 |

As the presence of gangs increased inside prison, so too did the number of rule violations. Institutional misconduct is higher in correctional facilities that have a more pronounced gang problem. Also, one state dummy variable was significant at explaining the variance in mean rule violations across prisons. In particular, the mean level of misconduct reported by subjects in Kentucky was lower than the average degree of misconduct among respondents in the other states.

In sum, table 6.7 reveals the reduced contextual model for rule violations. At Level 1, inmate age, prior gang involvement, perception of crowding, prison friendships, deviant prison associates, and prisonization were all significant at the .05 level even when Level 2 variables were included in the model. Two macro variables accounted for some of the Level 2 variance in rule violations.

## HLM Versus OLS: A Comparison of Regression Techniques

Several aspects of the analysis seem to warrant a comparison of hierarchical linear modeling with traditional ordinary least squares regression. The relatively low intraclass correlations obtained for both dependent variables (i.e., prisonization and institutional misconduct) call into question the use of HLM. In particular, it is difficult to justify the need for contextual analysis when only about 5 percent of the variation in prisonization occurred at Level 2. Even more problematic was the change in significance for this variation when independent micro antecedents were introduced at the random coefficients stage. Given these considerations, the results obtained from HLM were compared with the results obtained from traditional regression analyses.

### An OLS Regression of Prisonization
The results of ordinary least squares regression of prisonization appear in Table 6.8. Several micro antecedents had significant effects on prisonization. As age increased, prisonization lessened. Nonwhites had a mean score of about 1.4 points lower than whites. Subjects who disclosed prior gang involvement scored about 3 points higher on the index than respondents who reported no prior gang activities before incarceration. As situational problems encountered inside prison increased, so too did prisonization. The perception of crowding was also positively associated with prisonization. Both general definitions toward the rules and religious involvement predicted lower degrees of prisonization. In particular, subjects who reported involvement in religious activities during the past year scored about 3.5 points lower on the prisonization index than respondents who had not participated in religious services. When compared with HLM, the direction and general magnitude of the effects obtained from OLS regression are almost identical. Only the values on the coefficients are slightly off. For example, the effects on prisonization of

Table 6.8
Prisonization Regressed on Individual and Institutional Variables

| Variable | Unstandardized Coefficient | Standard Error | t-Ratio |
|---|---|---|---|
| Constant | 40.515** | .293 | 138.17 |
| Inmate Age | -201** | .031 | -6.39 |
| Race | -1.449* | .610 | -2.38 |
| Prior Gang Involvement | 3.012** | .934 | 3.23 |
| Situational Problems | .186** | .031 | 5.99 |
| Perception of Crowding | 1.066** | .288 | 3.70 |
| General Definitions | -.505** | .084 | -6.03 |
| Religious Involvement | -3.454** | .600 | -5.76 |
| Prison Age | -.026 | .014 | -1.85 |
| Prison Security Level | 3.332** | .978 | 3.41 |
| Prison Percent Under 25 | -6.068 | 4.413 | -1.65 |
| $R^2$ | .204 | | |

*significant at the .05 level
**significant at the .01 level

race and general definitions were slightly greater according to HLM. However, OLS regression yielded slightly higher coefficients for age, prior gang involvement, situational problems, perception of crowding, and religious involvement.

In regard to the Level 2 antecedents of prisonization, OLS regression was remarkably similar to HLM. The prison's age, its security level, the percentage of inmates under 25 years old were all significantly predictive (i.e., at the .10 level) of higher prisonization. In particular, as the age of the institution increased, prisonization declined. Also, using OLS regression techniques, the average prisonization score was 3.33 points higher in maximum security institutions than in non-max facilities. HLM yield a coefficient of 3.47, suggesting that the mean prisonization score was 3.47 points higher in maximum security prisons than in non-max institutions. Furthermore, both HLM and OLS regression indicated that prisonization declined as the percentage of inmates under 25 years old increased. All Level 2 coefficients obtained from HLM were slightly higher than those from OLS regression. This may indicate that HLM better estimated Level 2 parameters than OLS regression.

Also, as a note of comparison, traditional regression analyses provide an $R^2$ statistic that basically is an estimation of the amount of variance in the dependent measure that is explained by the model. The integrated model, including both micro and macro antecedents, explained 20.4 percent of the variance in prisonization. The adjusted $R^2$ for this model was .196.

## An OLS Regression of Rule Violations

Table 6.9 displays the results of the ordinary least squares regression of rule violations. The direction and general magnitude of all micro and macro predictors of rule violations inside prison were quite parallel. Both HLM and OLS regression revealed that as inmates age, rule violations decrease. The coefficients for this variable were identical across methodologies. Likewise, subjects reporting gang involvement on the street had higher mean levels of misconduct than did respondents not revealing prior gang activity. A greater effect was derived from OLS regression for prior gang involvement. Visits from family and friends appeared to decrease rule infractions, whereas prisonization increased institutional misconduct. The effect was larger in OLS and significant at the .05 alpha level, whereas it was only significant at the .10 level according to HLM. Prison friendships were inversely associated with rule violations according to both HLM and OLS regression, although the coefficient was higher according to OLS. Both statistical techniques also revealed that as the number of a subject's deviant prison associates inside prison increased, so too did his extent of institutional misconduct. However, the coefficients on this variable were identical in HLM and OLS. Lastly, both types of regression indicated that prisonization was related to institutional misconduct, but OLS estimated a larger coefficient.

The effects of Level 2 variables on institutional misconduct were similar for both HLM and OLS regression. In particular, rule violations

Table 6.9
Rule Violations Regressed on Individual and Institutional Variables

| Variable | Unstandardized Coefficient | Standard Error | t-Ratio |
|---|---|---|---|
| Constant | .582** | .021 | 27.66 |
| Inmate Age | -.011** | .002 | -4.95 |
| Prior Gang Involvement | .299** | .068 | 4.42 |
| Visits from Family and Friends | -.028* | .014 | -1.96 |
| Prison Friendships | -.064** | .022 | -2.98 |
| Deviant Prison Associates | .039** | .012 | 3.24 |
| Perception of Crowding | .056** | .022 | 2.62 |
| Prisonization | .006** | .002 | 2.99 |
| Prison Gang Presence | 1.785** | .002 | 3.44 |
| Kentucky | -2.10** | .045 | -4.69 |
| | | | |
| $R^2$ | .142 | | |

*significant at the .05 level
**significant at the .01 level

increased as did the gang presence inside prison. In general, both HLM and OLS regression point to the importance of a gang presence in explaining misconduct inside prison. However, HLM estimated a larger effect for gang presence. Finally, on average, inmates in Kentucky had a lower degree of misconduct inside prison than subjects in the other states. The coefficient for the Kentucky dummy variable was larger in OLS regression as compared with HLM.

As one final point of comparison, ordinary least squares regression yielded an $R^2$ statistic that estimated the amount of variance in rule violations which was explained by my integrated theoretical model (i.e., the combination of deprivation and importation theory). The conceptual model, including both micro and macro factors, only explained about 14.2

percent of the variance in rule violations. The adjusted $R^2$ for this model was .141. This low $R^2$ suggests that an alternate theory may offer a better explanation for institutional misconduct than the prisonization hypothesis.

## A Multilevel Analysis of Prisonization

The goal of this chapter was to analyze prison life from a multilevel perspective. Multilevel modeling revealed that both prisonization and its consequence (i.e., institutional misconduct) significantly vary across correctional facilities, albeit this variation was quite small. Prisonization was also significantly associated with institutional misconduct and appeared to mediate the effects of other Level 1 variables on misconduct. Further tests indicated that the Level 2 variance component for prisonization became non-significant once micro antecedents were introduced into the random coefficients model. The low intraclass correlations coupled with the disappearance of significant Level 2 variation prompted a comparison of hierarchical linear modeling with traditional ordinary least squares regression models. The comparison revealed that OLS regression techniques did as good a job at estimating the effects on prisonization of micro and macro antecedents as hierarchical linear modeling. The results from OLS regression were virtually identical to those obtained from HLM. However, for this analysis, HLM would have been beneficial at shedding light on the cross-level interactions between individual and institutional factors. Unfortunately, no such interactions were observed in the analysis.

# CHAPTER 7

# The Implications of A Multilevel Analysis of Prisonization

This project has primarily been a contextual analysis of prison life. The goal was to explore the antecedents and consequences of prisonization from a multilevel perspective. The main assumption underlying the current project has been that individual characteristics alone cannot explain inmate code adoption and subsequent misconduct. Contextual features, or qualities of the correctional institutions in which inmates serve their sentences, are essential to a complete understanding of social relations inside prison. As such, the context of corrections may be important in two specific ways. First, it may directly affect an inmate's likelihood of prisonization. In other words, context may have main effects that are independent of personal traits. Secondly, contextual features may interact with individual characteristics. This may cause individual factors to vary in their effects, according to the context in which they occur.

**A Review of the Findings**

Several hypotheses were confirmed by this contextual analysis. First, the significant intraclass correlations obtained for both dependent variables (i.e., prisonization and rule violations) established that the mean levels of each varied across prison contexts, confirming the first two Level 1 hypotheses. This is a finding in and of itself because it suggests that prisonization and misconduct are not uniform across all correctional facilities. Rather, the levels of each fluctuate across different prisons.

Prisonization
Several Level 1 importation factors affected prisonization in unexpected ways. When controlling for all other variables, as the age of the inmate increased, the degree of prisonization declined. It was expected that older convicts would be more prisonized than younger inmates when, in fact, younger subjects reported higher degrees of prisonization than did older respondents. Additionally, it was expected that nonwhite inmates would

be more highly prisonized than white inmates. However, the results indicated that the mean prisonization score for nonwhites was almost 1.5 points lower than the average score for whites. However, as expected, the degree of prisonization was higher for inmates who disclosed gang involvement prior to incarceration. Specifically, the prisonization score for inmates with a prior history of gang activity was almost 3 points higher than the score for prisoners with no prior indication of gang involvement. Neither prior incarcerations nor prior violence were predictive of prisonization. In sum, relationships between prisonization and three Level 1 importation variables were established, albeit two (i.e., age and race) were in the direction opposite of that which was expected. Moreover, it is important to note that the effects on prisonization of these importation variables did not vary across institutional contexts.

Prisonization was also associated with two micro-level factors from the deprivation model. In particular, the Level 1 hypothesis concerning crowding was supported by this multilevel analysis. As an inmate's perception of crowding increased, so too did his prisonization score. Also as expected, net all other effects, as a subject's situational problems increased inside prison, his degree of prisonization was elevated. In this analysis, sentence length, time served, outside contacts, prison friendships, and deviant prison associates were all unrelated to prisonization. As with the importation variables, the effects of deprivation measures on prisonization did not vary across correctional facilities.

Furthermore, two control variables were found to be important predictors of prisonization. Specifically, as a respondent's general prosocial definitions of the rules increased, his degree of prisonization declined. Unexpectedly, the effect on prisonization of these prosocial attitudes varied across correctional facilities. Additionally, when controlling for all other variables, the average prisonization score for subjects who attended religious services in prison during the last year was over 3 points lower than the mean score of survey respondents who had not participated in religious programming. However, the effect on prisonization of religious involvement did not vary across institutional contexts. Neither self-esteem nor coping difficulties affected prisonization.

The findings from hierarchical linear modeling also shed light on several Level 2 hypotheses. As expected, the average prisonization score in maximum security correctional facilities was over 3 points higher than the mean score in non-max prisons. Another finding also supported an association between prisonization and a prison-level feature. In particular, as the age of the prison increased, prisonization inside decreased. Although this result was in the direction opposite of that predicted in the hypotheses, it still establishes the fact that institutional features directly affect individual outcomes. Perhaps newer prisons are actually more custodial than older institutions (e.g., as in the case of the recent building of super-max facilities). If correct, then this explains why prisonization is more pronounced in newer correctional institutions. No other Level 2 variables significantly predicted prisonization scores. Likewise, the hypothesis concerning cross-level interaction was not substantiated. That is, deprivation variables at the prison-level did not intensify the effects on prisonization of individual-level deprivations.

## Institutional Misconduct

Only two micro-level importation variables affected institutional misconduct. The results from the multilevel analysis revealed that as the age of the inmate increased, institutional misconduct decreased. Also, subjects who reported a history of gang activity engaged in more rule violations inside prison than did respondents with no prior gang involvement. Race, prior incarcerations, and prior violence did not affect the amount of rule violations. Moreover, no measures of importation varied in their effects on institutional misconduct.

At least three Level 1 deprivation variables affected institutional misconduct. In particular, as a respondent's perception of crowding increased, so too did his number of rule violations. Also, as the number of deviant prison associates increased, a subject's involvement in institutional misconduct escalated. An unexpected finding was uncovered regarding misconduct and prison friendships. Specifically, an inmate with many close friendships inside prison reported few rule violations. No other deprivation variables were predictive of institutional misconduct at the micro-level. Likewise, the effects of deprivation variables on misconduct did not vary across prisons.

Only two Level 2 variables had significant main effects on institutional misconduct. In particular, as the gang presence inside prison increased, individual acts of institutional misconduct increased. Also, on average, subjects in Kentucky reported fewer instances of rule violations than survey participants in the other states. No other Level 2 factors significantly predicted rule violations in prison. Moreover, the hypothesis concerning cross-level interaction was not substantiated. That is, deprivation variables at the prison-level did not intensify the effects on institutional misconduct of individual-level deprivations.

**Theoretical Contributions**

There are a number of theoretical implications suggested by the findings of this research report. First and foremost, prisonization seems to continue to occur inside modern correctional institutions. Inmates still seem to collectively adhere to a set of attitudes or a code that addresses their problems (e.g., the perception of crowding and other situational issues such as missing somebody, being bored, feeling sexually frustrated, etc.). However, the antecedents of prisonization are less similar to those specified by Clemmer (1940) and more similar to ones advanced by Irwin (1980).

In particular, Clemmer (1940) proposed that longer sentences, an unstable personality, a lack of outside contacts, greater integration into prison groups, blind acceptance of prison dogmas, chance, abnormal sexual behavior, and gambling contributed to prisonization. None of these factors, with the exception of chance (i.e., error), significantly predicted taking on the inmate code in greater or less degree in this sample of twenty-first century prisoners. Irwin (1980), on the other hand, has implied that if prisonization still exists in modern correctional facilities, then it must be associated with gang membership. Stevens (1997) has also suggested that prisonization is more pronounced among gang members. Indeed, the results of the current project confirm the link between prisonization and gang involvement prior to incarceration. However, at the macro level, the gang presence inside prison was unrelated to prisonization. This suggests that it is not the overall presence of prison gangs per se that affects prisonization, but rather an individual's gang-related socialization experiences on the street or in a prior institutional setting such as juvenile detention (Stevens, 1997).

The current project provides some support for the integration of indigenous influence theory (i.e., deprivation) with cultural drift theory (i.e., importation) when explaining prisonization. In fact, the conceptual model included variables from theories of importation and deprivation. This model, supported by an integrated deprivation-importation theory, is useful in explaining subcultural responses such as prisonization. Moreover, prisonization was related to institutional misconduct even when controlling for other variables.

This study also revealed that prisonization and misconduct are not uniform across correctional facilities. The mean levels of these individual-level processes varied significantly across prison contexts. Furthermore, they were influenced by both micro and macro features. However, micro variables were much more important in explaining social relations inside prison than macro factors. In a sense, the current project confirms the conceptualization of subcultural formation advanced by Cohen (1955/1997). He proposed that subcultural formation occurs in response to the problems associated with an actor's frame of reference as opposed to the problems presented by the context itself. In this study, the Level 1 measure of crowding (i.e., the subject's perception of crowding) was significantly related to prisonization while the Level 2 crowding variable (i.e., inmate population/operating capacity) was unrelated to prisonization. At least for crowding, it seems that an individual's perception or frame of reference is more important than the institutional milieu when explaining subcultural responses (i.e., prisonization).

Lastly, this analysis did not reveal any cross-level interactions in regard to prisonization or misconduct. In fact, only one micro-level coefficient (i.e., the slope of general definitions) varied in its effect on prisonization across contexts. Furthermore, no interaction with any of the Level 2 research variables could significantly account for this variation. The absence of cross-level interactions seems to suggest that the contextual features of correctional facilities do not influence the individual-level relationships inside prison to any substantial degree. In other words, the prison contexts in this study had only main effects on individual-level phenomena. The current project casts serious doubt on statements that imply a cross-level interaction between personal qualities and institutional features. For example, Hofer (1988) has suggested that "[the] matching of the penitentiary environment with pathological aspects of the antisocial personality provides an unconscious, characterological appeal to many inmates, promoting expression of rebellious 'prisonized' attitudes and increasing the chance of recidvism" (p. 95). These findings suggest that this prisoner-prison *matching* simply does not occur. In this sample, individual-level effects were not exacerbated by institutional factors.

In sum, the current project makes quite a few theoretical contributions. First, it appears as if prisonization still occurs inside modern correctional facilities. However, the nature of this social process has changed somewhat since it was first described by Clemmer (1940). Secondly, the results confirm that an integrated deprivation-importation model is useful in explaining prisonization. Also, variables from both Level 1 (i.e., prisoners) and Level 2 (i.e., prisons) are needed in order to fully understand social relations inside prison, albeit the characteristics of inmates are more explanatory than prison-level factors. Lastly, the lack of any cross-level interactions implies that prison contexts do not influence social relationships on the inside to any significant degree.

## Methodological Contributions

The findings also point to several methodological implications. From a practical standpoint, similar results obtained from OLS regression and HLM suggest that OLS regression may be just as effective at determining the fixed main effects on prisonization of both Level 1 and Level 2 antecedents. The OLS regression coefficients did not appear to differ from those obtained by HLM in direction or magnitude. The current project also seemed to indicate that the relationships at Level 1 were the most meaningful. Indeed, if this is the case, then OLS regression may be more appropriate than HLM for analyzing social relations inside prison.

However, OLS regression cannot illustrate how dependent events (i.e., prisonization and misconduct) vary from prison to prison. HLM remains a superior analytic technique for establishing intraclass correlations, as well as identifying micro antecedents that vary in their effects. In fact, HLM showed which Level 1 effects varied across prisons. HLM could have also illustrated which Level 2 variables explained those cross-level effects. In sum, HLM offers promise for correctional research. HLM is particularly useful in understanding cross-level variation in individual processes.

## Limitations

While the current project was based on sound methodology, some limitations must still be addressed. First, the mixed sampling strategy could have possibly introduced strong bias into the sample. In particular, the sub-sample of Ohioans may be particularly problematic since it was completely non-random. This calls into question the validity and generalizability of the results. Furthermore, only prisons in Kentucky, Tennessee, and Ohio were sampled. The geographical proximity of these states may have influenced the results and weakened the multilevel analyses by decreasing heterogeneity between Level 2 units (i.e., prisons). The extent to which the findings are generalizable to prisons and prisoners in other geographical locations is uncertain. In fact, the results may only apply to the surveyed inmates in this sample of prisons.

Lastly, this study does not completely settle several disputes in correctional research. Some scholars have suggested that the concept of prisonization is no longer useful in understanding individual adaptation to imprisonment. More generally, others maintain that concerns over institutional adaptation are irrelevant since contemporary correctional policy tends to favor control and custody rather than rehabilitation. However, results from the current project seem to indicate that prisonization is a bonafide social phenomenon that is particularly real in its consequences. Furthermore, prisonization predicts rule violations inside the facility and partially mediates the effects on institutional misconduct of both deprivation and importation variables. Yet, the results also suggested that the notion of prisonization has changed since it was first conceptualized over sixty years ago. In particular, the strongest antecedents of prisonization are now individual characteristics such as race, prior gang activity, and perceptions of deprivation.

## Policy Implications

Although the current project has been an academic endeavor, it has some clear policy implications. As noted in the first chapter, both the extent and cost of imprisonment are increasing in the United States. In order to address these trends, it is important to target social processes that may be contributing to imprisonment and recidivism. As demonstrated by the current project, prisonization is associated with institutional misconduct. Prisonization may also related to a variety of social maladies, including drug abuse, unemployment, parole violations, and recidivism (Clemmer, 1940; Homant, 1984; Peat & Winfree, 1992; Winfree, Mays, Crowley, and Peat, 1994; Zingraff, 1975).

It is reasonable to believe that these consequences of prisonization have contributed in some form to the escalation of imprisonment in the U.S. As such, policies that attempt to disrupt the prisonization process may, then, diminish the rate of further imprisonment in this country. Although inmate characteristics (i.e., age, race, prior gang involvement, etc.) associated with prisonization are impossible to change, the situational deprivations and institutional features that contribute to the phenomenon may merit re-consideration. For example, if it is known that prisonization increases as inmates perceive more situational problems and crowding, then attempts to relieve these deprivations may result in less prisonization, decreased misconduct, increased adjustment, and possibly lower rates of recidivism.

Lastly, according to the National Institute of Corrections (1991), "gangs are known to perpetuate criminal activity, and they threaten violence and total disruption of an institution" (p. 1). The current study demonstrated that as the percentage of inmates who reported gang activity inside prison increased, the number of rule violations reported by survey participants also increased. In other words, the presence of gangs at the macro-level contributed to misconduct at the micro-level. In regard to prisonization, individual prior gang membership was more influential; prison-level gang activity was unrelated to prisonization. Perhaps this points to the importance of pre-prison socialization experiences in shaping an individual's attitudes about authority. As far as gangs are concerned, pre-prison involvement at the micro-level was associated with prisonized attitudes, while gang activity at the macro-level was related with illicit behavior (i.e., rule violations) on the inside. In sum, it appears as if cultural gang-related experiences outside prison may shape attitudes, and situational gang-related deprivations inside prison may influence behaviors.

The National Institute of Corrections recommends a number of gang control strategies, including housing options, out-of-state transfers, separate facilities, isolation of gang leaders, targeting individual gang members, control of inmate programs and jobs, and prosecution of gang-related activity. This research supports measures that directly reduce the presence of gangs inside prison such as the dispersion of known gang members throughout the system, as opposed to concentrating them together in a separate facility. As such, of the above options, out-of-state transfers may be the most effective gang control strategy in this case. Regardless, the results of this study should be replicated before any policies are changed or enacted.

**Directions for Future Research**

Future research should explore additional theoretical, methodological, and practical avenues. In particular, the conceptual model used in the current project was based upon theories of deprivation and importation. However, it only explained about twenty percent of the variation in prisonization. The integrated deprivation-importation model with prisonization included as a predictor only explained about fourteen percent of the variation in rule violations. This research suggests that neither indigenous influence theory nor cultural drift theory provides a sufficient explanation of prisonization or institutional misconduct. Instead of refining models of deprivation and importation, future studies should integrate theories from multiple disciplines in order to explain social processes (e.g., prisonization, institutional misconduct, suicide, dependency, etc.) inside prison.

Furthermore, perhaps conceptualizing prisonization as a rational and subcultural response is inaccurate. Indeed, the theories used in this study (i.e., socialization theory, subcultural theory, importation, and deprivation) present a very functional and socialized account of life inside prison. However, it may be that prison life is less rational, less socialized, and less functional. Life inside prison actually may be more basic and reactionary. Furthermore, prisonization and the inmate code may involve attitudes that are not localized inside correctional facilities at all, but are widespread throughout society. For example, children in elementary, middle, and high school routinely stick together and avoid snitching when one of their peers has committed a deviant act that has been detected by their teacher. Whistle-blowing is far more common among conventional adults. When conceptualized in this manner, resistance to authority and in-group solidarity seem rather *immature*.

Currently, certain developmental theories are popular within mainstream criminology (see Loeber & LeBlanc, 1990; Nagan, Farrington, & Moffitt, 1995). Yet over forty years ago, Sullivan, Grant, and Grant (1957) proposed that deviance results from the interrupted development of interpersonal maturity and related social skills. It may be that the inmate code is simply an expression of values learned during an early and possibly interrupted stage of development. In fact, certain attitudes (i.e., resistance to authority and in-group solidarity) are typically viewed as immature by adults, but are quite prevalent among younger members of society. In fact, age was inversely related to prisonization in the current project. Furthermore, Stevens' (1997) study of prison gang members supports a quasi-developmental perspective. Stevens discussed a developmental process (i.e., juvenilization) that begins at juvenile training facilities and results in adult entry into the prison gang world. Additionally, if the tenets of the inmate code are related to a developmental phase, then such approaches may be applied to the study of prison life in order to predict who will become prisonized and maladjusted once inside. In particular, future studies of prison life may wish to examine events further back in the life-course (e.g., family disruption, undeveloped social skills, lack of supervision, inconsistent punishment, parental rejection, etc.) in order to explain attitudes and behaviors inside correctional facilities. Of course, this would require researchers to rely upon recalled memories or longitudinal tracking of at-risk children.

By embarking on this discussion of developmental approaches, the point has been to illustrate how extant theories that are often used in correctional research may be outdated. Certainly, the correlates of prisonization that Clemmer (1940) identified are no longer accurate. Rather than conceptualizing groups of prisoners as subcultures, their adjustment to imprisonment as a rational and functional response, and the prisonization process as socialization, perhaps inmates should now be seen as individuals with similar life-course trajectories who may react to incarceration in developmentally immature ways. Perhaps there is no socialization or enculturation inside prison. In fact, the notion of a *society* of captives or a prison *community* may no longer be appropriate. Simply put, it may be time to expand traditional thinking about life inside prison.

In addition to these theoretical suggestions, subsequent research should also consider alternative methodologies. This research is one of the first studies of prison life to use hierarchical linear modeling (HLM) techniques. Ideally, prisonization and other social processes inside prison should be measured at several different times. As such, growth-curve analysis may be an appropriate methodology to apply to the study of prisonization and related processes. Additionally, analytic techniques that combine hierarchical linear modeling with structural equation modeling or path analysis may better estimate the effects and consequences of attitudes and behaviors inside prison. Of course, when using these quantitative techniques, larger samples especially at the macro-level would also yield better results. Finally, as an alternative strategy, qualitative methodologies (e.g., focus groups, intensive interviews, participant observation, etc.) may help researchers more completely understand the social processes of life inside prison as well as the effects of prison context.

Moreover, future multilevel investigations of prison life may wish to consider outcomes other than those (i.e., prisonization and misconduct) examined in this study. It would be interesting and possibly quite instructive to perform a follow-up study with subjects after release to determine if prisonization scores predict other social problems such as drug use and abuse, unemployment, and undetected deviance. Furthermore, if the data are ever available, an analysis of the relationship between prisonization and recidivism is obviously needed.

# BIBLIOGRAPHY

Adamek, R. J. & Dager, E. Z. (1968). Social structure, identification and change in a treatment-oriented institution. *American Sociological Review* (33), 931-944.

Aday, R. H. & Webster, E. L. (1979). Aging in prison: The development of a preliminary model. *Offender Rehabilitation* (3), 271-282.

Akers, R. L. (1997). *Criminological theories: Introduction and evaluation* (2nd ed.). Los Angeles: Roxbury Publishing Company.

Akers, R. L. (1998). *Social learning and social structure: A general theory of crime and deviance.* Boston: Northeastern University Press.

Akers, R. L, Hayner, N. S., & Gruninger, W. (1977). Prisonization in five countries: Type of prison and inmate characteristics. *Criminology* (14), 527-554.

Alexander, J.C. (1987). *Twenty lectures: Sociological theory since World War II.* New York: Columbia University Press.

Allen, F. A. (1981). *The decline of the rehabilitative ideal.* New Haven, Connecticut: Yale University Press.

Allport, G. W. (1968). The historical background of modern social psychology. In G. Lindzey & E. Aronson (Eds.), *The handbook of social psychology* (pp. 1-80). Reading, MA: Addison-Wesley.

Alpert, G. P. (1979). Patterns of change in prisonization: A longitudinal analysis. *Criminal Justice and Behavior* (6), 159-174.

Ambrosio, T. & Schiraldi, V. (1997). *From classrooms to cell blocks: A national perspective.* Washington, D.C.: Justice Policy Institute.

Anderson, L. C. (2000). *Voices from a southern prison.* Athens, GA: University of Georgia Press.

Atchley, R. & McCabe, M. (1968). Socialization in correctional communities: A replication. *American Sociological Review* (33), 312-323.

Bachman, R. & Paternoster, R. (1997). *Statistical methods for criminology and criminal justice.* New York: McGraw-Hill Companies Inc.

Bacon, M. H. (1985). *The quiet rebels: The story of the Quakers in America.* Philadelphia: New Society Publishers.

Becker, H. S. (1964). Personal change in adult life. *Sociometry* (27), 40-53.

Berger, P. L. & Berger, B. (1972). *Sociology: A biographical approach.* New York: Basic Books, Ltd.

Berk, B. B. (1966). Organizational goals and inmate organization. *American Journal of Sociology* (71), 522-534.

Blumstein, A., & Beck, A. J. (1999). Population growth in U.S. prisons, 1980-1996. In M. T. Tonry & J. Petersilia (Eds.), *Prisons* (pp. 17-61). Chicago: The University of Chicago Press.

Bonta, J. & Gendreau, P. (1990). Reexamining the cruel and unusual punishment of prison life. *Law and Human Behavior* (14), 347-372.

Brawell, M. & Gillespie, W. (1999). From a peacemaking perspective, is individual change more important than social change? In J. R. Fuller & E. W. Hickey (Eds.), *Controversial issues in criminology* (pp. 110-119). Boston: Allyn and Bacon.

Bryk, A. S. & Raudenbush, S. W. (1992). *Hierarchical linear models: Applications and data analysis methods.* Newbury Park: Sage Publications.

Bukstel, L. H. & Kilmann, P. R. (1980). Psychological effects of imprisonment on confined individuals. *Psychological Bulletin* (88), 469-493.

Bureau of Justice Statistics. (1997). *Census of state and federal correctional facilities.* Washington, D.C.: U.S. Department of Justice, Bureau of Justice Statistics.

Bureau of Justice Statistics. (1999). *State prison expenditures, 1996* (NCJ 172211). Washington, D.C.: U.S. Department of Justice, Bureau of Justice Statistics.

Bureau of Justice Statistics. (2000). *Prisoners in 1999* (NCJ 183476). Washington, D.C.: U.S. Department of Justice, Bureau of Justice Statistics.

Burton, V. L., Cullen, F. T., Evans, D., & Dunaway, G. (1994). Reconsidering strain theory: Operationalization, rival theories, and adult criminality. *Journal of Quantitative Criminology* (10), 213-239.

Bush, D. M. & Simmons, R. G. (1992). Socialization processes over the life course. In M. Rosenberg & R. H. Turner (Eds.), *Social psychology: Sociological Perspectives* (pp.133-164). New Brunswick, NJ: Transaction Publishers.

Calhoun, J. B. (1962). Population density and social pathology. *Scientific American* (206), 139-148.

Caplow, T. & Simon, J. (1999). Understanding prison policy and population trends. In M. T. Tonry & J. Petersilia (Eds.), *Prisons* (pp. 63-120). Chicago: The University of Chicago Press.

Chernoff, H. A., Kelly, C. M., & Kroger, J. R. (1996). The politics of crime. *Harvard Law Journal* (33), 527-578.

Clausen, J. A. (1968). *Socialization and society.* Boston: Little, Brown and Company.

Clemmer, D. (1940). *The prison community.* Boston: Christopher Publishing Company.

Clemmer, D. (1950). Observations on imprisonment as a source of criminality. *Journal of Criminal Law & Criminology* (41), 311-319.

Clemmer, D. (1958). *The prison community* (Re-issued edition). New York: Rinehart.

Cohen, A. K. (1976). Prison violence: A sociological perspective. In A. K. Cohen, G. F. Cole, & R. G. Bailey (Eds.), *Prison violence* (pp. 3-22). Lexington, MA: Lexington Books.

Cohen, A. K. (1997). A general theory of subcultures. In K. Gelder & S. Thornton (Eds.), *The subcultures reader* (pp.44-54). London: Routledge. (Original work published 1955)

Cooley, C. H. (1964). *Human nature and the social order.* New York: Shocken Books, Inc.

Cox, V. C., Paulus, P. B., & McCain, G. (1984). Prison crowding research: The relevance for prison housing standards and a general approach regarding crowding phenomena. *American Psychologist* (39), 1148-1160.

Cullen, F. T., Skovron, S. E., Scott, J. E. and Burton, V. S. (1990). Public support for correctional treatment: The tenacity of rehabilitative ideology. *Criminal Justice and Behavior* (17), 6-18.

Curry, L. (2001). Excerpts form the journal of Louis Curry, Chief Warden. [On-line]. Available: http://www.angelfire.com/ky/ksp/KSPhistory.html (Original work published in 1895).

Dale, M. (1976). Barriers to the rehabilitation of ex-offenders. *Crime and Delinquency* (22), 322-337.

Durkheim, E. (1964). *The rules of the sociological method.* New York: Free Press. (Original work published in 1895)

Eckl, C. (1998). The cost of corrections. *State Legislatures* (24), 30-33.

Faine, J. R. (1973). A self-consistency approach to prisonization. *The Sociological Quarterly* (14), 576-588.

Farrington, D. (1973). Self-reports of deviant behavior: Predictive and stable? *Journal of Criminal Law and Criminology* (64), 99-110.

Farrington, D. P. & Nuttall, C. P. (1980). Prison size, overcrowding, prison violence, and recidivism. *Journal of Criminal Justice* (8), 221-231.

Flynn, E. E. (1976). The ecology of prison violence. In A. K. Cohen, G. F. Cole, & R. G. Bailey (Eds.), *Prison violence* (pp. 115-134). Lexington, MA: Lexington Books.

Garabedian, P. G. (1963). Social roles and processes of socialization in the prison community. *Social Problems* (11), 139-152.

Gecas, V. (1992). Contexts of socialization. In M. Rosenberg & R. H. Turner (Eds.), *Social psychology: Sociological perspectives* (pp.164-199). New Brunswick, NJ: Transaction Publishers.

Gendreau, P. (1998). The principles of effective intervention with offenders. In A. T. Harland (Ed.), *Choosing correctional options that work* (pp. 117-130). Thousand Oaks: Sage Publications.

Giddings, F. H. (1895). Is the term 'social classes' a scientific category? *Proceedings of the National Conference of Charities and Correction, New Haven,* 110-116.

Goffman, E. (1961). *Asylums.* New York: Anchor Books/Doubleday.

Gordon, M. M. (1997). The concept of the sub-culture and its application. In K. Gelder & S. Thornton (Eds.), *The subcultures reader* (pp.40-43). London: Routledge. (Original work published 1947)

Grusky, O. (1959). Organizational goals and the behavior of informal leaders. *American Journal of Sociology* (65), 59-67.

Hagan, J. & Dinovitzer, R. (1999). Collateral consequence of imprisonment for children, communities, and prisoners. In M. T. Tonry & J. Petersilia (Eds.), *Prisons* (pp. 121-162). Chicago: The University of Chicago Press.

Haney, C. (1997). Psychology and the limits to prison pain: Confronting the coming crisis in eighth amendment law. *Psychology, Public Policy, and Law* (3), 499-588.

Haney, C. (1998). The past and future of U.S. prison policy: Twenty-five years after the Stanford Prison Experiment. *American Psychologist* (53), 709-727.

Hawkins, G. (1976). *The prison - policy and practice.* Chicago: University of Chicago Press.

Haynes, F. E. (1948). The sociological study of the prison community. *Journal of Criminal Law & Criminology* (39), 432-440.

Herskovits, M. J. (1949). *Man and his works: The science of cultural anthropology.* New York: Alfred A. Knopf.

Hofer, P. (1988). Prisonization and recidivism: A psychological perspective. *Interantional Journal of Offender Therapy and Comparative Criminology* (32), 95-106.

Homant, R. J. (1984). Employment of ex-offenders: the role of prisonization and self-esteem. *Journal of Counseling, Services, & Rehabilitation* (8), 5-24.

House, J. S. (1992). Social structure and personality. In M. Rosenberg & R. H. Turner (Eds.), *Social psychology: Sociological Perspectives* (pp.525-561). New Brunswick, NJ: Transaction Publishers.

Hunt, G., Riegel, S., Morales, T., & Waldorf, D. (1993). Changes in prison culture: Prison gangs and the case of the "pepsi generation". *Social Problems* (40), 398-409.

Inciardi, J. A., Lockwood, D., & Quinlan, J. A. (1993). Drug use in prison: Patterns, processes, and implications for treatment. *The Journal of Drug Issues* (23), 119-129.

Irwin, J. (1980). *Prisons in turmoil.* Boston: Little, Brown, and Company.

Irwin, J. (1997). Notes on the status of the concept subculture. In K. Gelder & S. Thornton (Eds.), *The subcultures reader* (pp.66-70). London: Routledge. (Original work published 1970)

Irwin, J. & Austin, J. (1994). *It's about time: America's Imprisonment Binge.* Belmont, CA: Wadsworth.

Irwin, J. & Cressey, D. R. (1962). Thieves, convicts, and the inmate culture. *Social Problems* (10), 142-155.

Jensen, G. F. & Jones, D. (1976). Perspectives on inmate culture: A study of women in prison. *Social Forces* (54), 590-603.

Johnson, R. (1996). *Hard time: Understanding and reforming the prison.* Belmont, CA: Wadsworth.

Johnson, R. (1997). Race, gender, and the American prison: Historical observations. In J. Pollock (Ed.), *Prisons: Today and tomorrow* (pp. 26-51). Gaithersburg, MD: Aspen Publishers, Inc.

Johnson, R. & Toch, H. (Eds.). (1982). *The pains of imprisonment.* Beverly Hills, CA: Sage Publications.

Kappeler, V. E., Blumberg, M., & Potter, G. W. (1996). Crime waves and crime fears: The myth of an American crisis. In V. E. Kappeler, M. Blumberg, & G. W. Potter (Eds.), *The mythology of crime and criminal justice* (pp.31-51). Prospect Heights, Illinois: Waveland Press.

Kennedy, D. B. & Kerber, A. (1973). *Resocialization: An American experiment.* New York: Behavioral Publications.

Kentucky Department of Correction. (2001). *KY Corrections Home Page.* [On-line]. Available: http://www.cor.state.ky.us.html.

Knox, G. (1981). Differential integration and job retention among ex-offenders. *Criminology* (18), 481-499.

Kornhauser, R. R. (1978). *Social sources of delinquency.* Chicago: University of Chicago Press.

Kreft, I. & De Leeuw, J. (1998). *Introducing multilevel modeling.* Thousand Oakes: Sage Publications.

Leahy, J. P. (1998). Coping strategies of prisoners in a maximum security prison: minimals, optimals and utilitarians. *Social Thought & Research* (21), 279-290.

Loeber, R. & LeBlanc, M. (1990). Toward a developmental criminology. In M. Tonry & N. Morris (Eds.), *Crime and justice* (12th ed., pp. 375-473). Chicago: University of Chicago Press.

Lombroso, C. & Ferrero, W. (1895). *The female offender.* London: Unwin Fisher.

MacKenzie, D. L., Robinson, J. W., & Campbell, C. S. (1989). Long-term incarceration of female offenders. *Criminal Justice and Behavior* (16), 223-238.

Maguire, K. & Pastore, A. L. (1997). *Sourcebook of Criminal Justice Statistics, 1996.* Washington, D.C.: U.S. Department of Justice, Bureau of Justice Statistics. Available online at http://www.albany.edu/sourcebook.3.

Marquis, K. H. & Ebener, P. A. (1981). *Quality of prisoner self-reports: Arrest and conviction response errors* (Report No. R-2637-DOJ). Santa Monica, CA: The Rand Corporation.

Martinson, R. (1974). What works? Questions and answers about prison reform. *The Public Interest* (35), 22-54.

Mathiesen, T. (1971). *Across the boundaries of organizations: An exploratory study of communication patterns in two penal institutions.* Berkeley, CA: Glendessary Press, Inc.

Matthews, R. (1999). *Doing time: An introduction to the sociology of imprisonment.* New York: St. Martin's Press, Inc.

Mattingly, T. (2001). Subcultural formation and the social crucible. Unpublished manuscript, University of Kentucky.

Mead, G. H. (1964). *On social psychology: Selected papers.* (A. Straus, Ed.). Chicago: University of Chicago Press.

Megargee, E. I. (1977). The association of population density, reduced space, and uncomfortable temperatures with misconduct in a prison community. *American Journal of Community Psychology* (5), 289-298.

Merton, R. K. (1968). *Social theory and social structure.* New York: The Free Press.

Miller, W. B. (1958). Lower class culture as a generating milieu of gang delinquency. *Journal of Social Issues* (15), 5-19.

Morris, T. & Morris, P. (1962). The experience of imprisonment. *British Journal of Criminology* (2), 337-360.

Nagin, D. S., Farrington, D. P., & Moffitt, T. E. (1995). Life-course trajectories of different types of offenders. *Criminology* (33), 1111-1139.

National Institute of Corrections. (1991). *Management strategies in disturbances and with gangs/disruptive groups.* Washington, DC: U.S. Department of Justice.

Ohio Department of Rehabilitation and Correction. (2001). *DRC Home Page.* [On-line]. Available: http://www.drc.state.oh.us.html.

Ohlin, L. E. (1956). *Sociology and the field of corrections.* New York: Russell Sage.

Parsons, T. (1937). *The structure of social action.* New York: McGraw-Hill.

Paulus, P., McCain, G., & Cox, V. (1973). A note on the use of prisons as environments for investigation of crowding. *Bulletin of the Psychonomic Society* (1), 427-428.

Peat, B. J. & Winfree, L. T. (1992). Reducing the intra-institutional effects of "prisonization": A study of the therapeutic community of drug-using inmates. *Criminal Justice and Behavior* (19), 206-225.

Petersilia, J. (1977). *The validity of criminality data derived from personal interviews* (Report No. P-5890). Santa Monica, CA: The Rand Corporation.

Platt, A. M. (1977). *The child savers: The invention of delinquency.* (2nd ed.). Chicago: The University of Chicago Press.

Pollock, J. (1997). The social world of the prisoner. In J. Pollock (Ed.), *Prisons: Today and tomorrow* (pp. 218-269). Gaithersburg, MD: Aspen Publishers, Inc.

Porporino, F. J. & Zamble, E. (1984). Coping with imprisonment. *Canadian Journal of Criminology* (26), 403-421.

Ramirez, J. (1984). Prisonization, staff, and inmates: Is it really about us versus them? *Criminal Justice and Behavior* (11), 423-460.

Richards, B. (1978). The experience of long-term imprisonment. *British Journal of Criminology* (18), 162-169.

Rosenberg, M. (1986). *Conceiving the self.* Malabar, FL: Krieger Publishing Company.

Schrag, C. (1961). Some foundations for a theory of correction. In D. Cressey (Ed.), *The prison: Studies in Institutional Organization and Change* (pp.309-358). New York: Holt, Rinehart, and Winston.

Schwartz, B. (1971). Pre-institutional vs. situational influence in a correctional community. *Journal of Criminal Law, Criminology, & Police Science* (62), 532-541.

Sewell, W. H. (1963). Some recent developments in socialization theory and research. *Annals of American Academy of Political and Social Sciences* (349), 163-181.

Shaw, C. (1930). *The jack-roller.* Chicago: University of Chicago Press.

Shibutani, T. (1956). Reference groups as perspectives. *American Journal of Sociology* (60), 562-569.

Sobell, L. C. & Sobell, M. B. (1975). Outpatient alcoholics give valid self-reports. *Journal of Nervous and Mental Diseases* (161), 33-42.

Sommer, R. (1971). The social psychology of the cell environment. *The Prison Journal* (51), 15-21.

Stevens, D. J. (1997). Origins and effects of prison drug gangs in north carolina. *Journal of Gang Research* (4), 23-35.

Stratton, J. (1967). Differential identification and attitudes toward the law. *Social Forces* (46), 256-263.

Street, D. (1966). The inmate group in custodial and treatment settings. *American Sociological Review* (30), 40-55.

Street, D., Vinter, R. D., & Perrow, C. (1966). *Organization for treatment: A comparative study of institutions for delinquents.* New York: The Free Press.

Sullivan, C., Grant, M. Q., Grant, J. D. (1957). The development of interpersonal maturity: Applications to delinquency. *Psychiatry* (20), 373-385.

Sutherland, E. (1937). *The professional thief.* Chicago: The University of Chicago Press.

Sykes, G. M. (1958). *The society of captives.* Princeton, New Jersey: Princeton University Press.

Sykes, G. M. & Messinger, S. (1960). The inmate social system. In R. Cloward (Ed.), *Theoretical studies in the social organization of the prison* (pp. 6-10). New York: Social Science Research Council.

Tennessee Department of Correction. (2001). *Tennessee Department of Correction Home Page.* [On-line]. Available: http://www.state.tn.us/correction.html.

Thomas, C. W. (1971). *Determinants of prisonization: A test of two analytical perspectives on adult socialization in total institutions.* Unpublished doctoral dissertation, University of Kentucky.

Thomas, C. W. (1977). Theoretical perspectives on prisonization: A comparison of the importation and deprivation models. *Journal of Criminal Law and Criminology* (68), 135-145.

Thomas, C. W. & Foster, S. C. (1972). Prisonization in the inmate contraculture. *Social Problems* (20), 229-239.

Thomas, C. W. & Petersen, D. M. (1977). *Prison organization and inmate subculture.* Indianapolis, IN: The Bobbs-Merrill Company, Inc.

Thomas, C. W., Petersen, D. M., & Zingraff, R. M. (1978). Structural and social psychological correlates of prisonization. *Criminology* (16), 383-393.

Thornton, R. & Nardi, P. M. (1975). The dynamics of role acquisition. *American Journal of Sociology* (80), 870-885.

Thrasher, F. M. (1927). *The gang.* Chicago: The University of Chicago Press.

Tittle, C. R. (1972). Institutional living and self esteem. *Social Problems* (20), 65-77.

Tittle, C. R. & Tittle, R. P. (1964). Social organization of prisoners: An empirical test. *Social Forces* (43), 215-221.

Toch, H. (1984). Quo vadis? *Canadian Journal of Criminology* (26), 511-516.

Von Hirsch, A. (1985). *Past or future crimes: Deservedness and dangerousness in the sentencing of criminals*. New Brunswick, NJ: Rutgers University Press.

Von Hirsch, A. (1998). Penal theories. In M. Tonry (Ed.), *The handbook of crime & punishment* (pp.659-682). Oxford: Oxford University Press.

Walker, S., Spohn, C., & DeLone, M. (1996). *The color of justice: Race, ethnicity, and crime in America*. Belmont, CA: Wadsworth Publishing Company.

Wellford, C. F. (1967). Factors associated with adoption of the inmate code: A study of normative socialization. *The Journal of Criminal Law, Criminology, and Police Science* (58). 197-203.

Wellford, C. F. (1973). Contact and commitment in a correctional community. *British Journal of Criminology* (13), 108-120.

Wheeler, S. (1961). Socialization in correctional communities. *American Sociological Review* (26), 679-712.

Wheeler, S. (1966). The structure of formally organized socialization settings. In O.G. Brim, Jr. & S. Wheeler (Eds.), *Socialization after childhood: Two essays* (pp. 51-116). New York: Wiley.

Wilcox Rountree, P. & Clayton, R. R. (1999). A contextual model of adolescent alcohol use across the rural-urban continuum. *Substance Use & Misuse* (34), 495-519.

Wilcox Rountree, P. & Land, K. C. (1996). Perceived risk versus fear of crime: Empirical evidence of conceptually distinct reactions in survey data. *Social Forces* (74), 1353-1376.

Wilder, H. A. (1965). The role of the 'rat' in the prison. *Federal Probation* (29), 44-60.

Wilson, T. P. (1968). Patterns of management and adaptations to organizational roles: A study of prison inmates. *American Journal of Sociology* (74), 146-157.

Wines, E. C. (1880). *The state of prisons and of child-saving institutions in the civilized world.* Cambridge: Harvard University Press.

Winfree, L. T., Mays, C. L., Crowley, J. E., Peat, B. J. (1994). Drug history and prisonization: Toward understanding variations in inmate institutional adaptations. *International Journal of Offender Therapy and Comparative Criminology* (38), 281-296.

Wooldredge, J., Griffin, T., & Pratt, T. (2001). Considering hierarchical models for research on inmate behavior: Predicting misconduct with multilevel data. *Justice Quarterly* (18), 203-231.

Zald, M. N. (1962). Organizational control structures in five correctional institutions. *American Journal of sociology* (68), 335-345.

Zingraff, M. T. (1975). Prisonization as an inhibitor of effective resocialization. *Criminology* (13), 366-388.

# Index